Simply the Best

Also by David Lloyd

Around the World in 80 Pints: My Search for Cricket's
Greatest Grounds

Last in the Tin Bath: The Autobiography

Simply the Best

THE GREAT CHARACTERS OF CRICKET FROM THE DON TO THE BEN

David Lloyd

with Richard Gibson

**SIMON &
SCHUSTER**

London · New York · Sydney · Toronto · New Delhi

First published in Great Britain by Simon & Schuster UK Ltd, 2020

Copyright © David Lloyd Productions Ltd, 2020

The right of David Lloyd to be identified as the author of this work has been
asserted in accordance with the Copyright, Designs and Patents Act, 1988.

1 3 5 7 9 10 8 6 4 2

Simon & Schuster UK Ltd
1st Floor
222 Gray's Inn Road
London WC1X 8HB

www.simonandschuster.co.uk
www.simonandschuster.com.au
www.simonandschuster.co.in

Simon & Schuster Australia, Sydney
Simon & Schuster India, New Delhi

The author and publishers have made all reasonable efforts to contact
copyright-holders for permission, and apologise for any omissions or errors in the
form of credits given. Corrections may be made to future printings.

A CIP catalogue record for this book is available from the British Library

Hardback ISBN: 978-1-4711-9002-5
eBook ISBN: 978-1-4711-9003-2

Typeset in Bembo by M Rules

Printed in the UK by CPI Group (UK) Ltd, Croydon, CR0 4YY

Lots of us lost a good friend in Bob Willis in December 2019 and this book is dedicated to him and the work of Prostate Cancer UK

CONTENTS

CHAPTER 1

The Don

Cricket has been my life and has introduced me to some weird and wonderful places over the past seven decades. It has taken me all over the world – from the cobbled streets of a Lancashire mill town to the banks of the bustling ones of the subcontinent. From matches played using borrowed kit to ones with sponsors adorning the front, back and sleeves of shirts.

However, although they have played their own part, what has made my cricketing life special is not the backdrops but the people within the dramas I have witnessed. Some I have got to know intimately: my childhood mentors, teammates, opponents, those I went on to coach, work colleagues on radio and television. Some less well or not at all: on-field adversaries who kept themselves to themselves, players who let their reputations talk for them, and those who I have observed from afar from behind the microphone.

This is a sport with plenty of room for everyone. From

those whose obsession with it has gone above and beyond the call of duty – someone like Steve Smith who would take his bat out to restaurants after a day's play, to the likes of Garry Sobers and Ian Botham, who often reported for duty at the ground in a morning not long after turning in from the night before. And some who were a combination of the two. Derek Randall, for example, used to get his wife to wear his new pads while she was ironing and doing other bits of house-work to break them in. But would play with a carefree spirit when he got out into the middle – chattering away, singing 'The Sun Has Got His Hat On', whistling and doffing his cap theatrically at Australian bowlers breathing fire.

The cricketers blessed with the greatest ability do not nec-essarily make the game's best characters, though, and in these pages I want to pay tribute to those that I have come across at grassroots level. To me, although it has a serious side and is one of great riches for those good enough to make it all the way to the top, this game has been a lot of fun.

I first learnt its potential for joy at Accrington Cricket Club, not only via those that competed with and against me, but through the support off the field. The spectators, the announcers, the groundsmen, the administration staff; the individuals that make cricket tick. It is a characteristic common to a lot of the folk that I include here. I trust you will forgive my indulgence in the lighter side of life. But I also hope to chronicle exactly what has made some of the finest performers cricket has welcomed to its global stage the players they became. What set them apart from their peers.

To this end, what better place to begin than with the most

esteemed player this sport has ever produced. Let's start with a touch of Tina Turner and, as the title of this book makes clear: Simply the Best. A man whose achievements are so familiar to the game's followers that, like a pop star, he can shed his surname and still be recognisable far and wide. Ladies and gentlemen, I give you the Don.

I had the privilege of a brief encounter – no more than a hello, really – with Sir Donald Bradman in 1974–75 while on an Ashes tour, when I was in the company of the England team manager, and his good pal, Alec Bedser.

However, a more formal meeting came in early 1977 when I was one of those invited to the first of two Centenary Tests. The first one commemorated the 100th anniversary of the first Test match held in Australia and Qantas, the country's flag-carrier airline, had invited all the England players who had played a minimum of four Test matches on Australian soil to attend.

Flown out from Heathrow on the eve of my 30th birthday as one of the Qantas guests, I travelled having scraped in by the barest of margins. I'd played exactly four Test matches there on the most recent MCC tour two years earlier, during which I had my testicles tickled by that friendly fast bowler Jeff Thomson.

It was a real honour to be included and Jack Bailey, the MCC's autocratic secretary of that period, clearly wanted us to pay due reverence to the magnitude of the occasion, assembling us ahead of departure, and with a particular emphasis on the younger end of the tour party – people like myself, John Lever, Ken Shuttleworth – made a speech in which he said, 'You know this is a trip on which even as non-playing members of England teams past, you will still be representing the country, and as such the behaviour has to be exemplary.' There followed a reminder to us 'young chaps' that this was not some sort of a holiday. Not a drink-a-thon.

Bailey was a highly principled man and always wanted the MCC to be projected in the best possible light. And that began with our conduct on this particular jumbo jet out of London, at the start of a 30-hour journey.

Although the great and the good are among us, we're all housed in Economy, including the 84-year-old Percy Fender, who had played first-class cricket before the Great War. Sat with a rug on his knee, he was accompanied by one of his younger family members, who stood in front of him, acting as a blockade, and announced to any member of the public who got too close: 'Mr Fender will not be signing today.'

Another of his generation, Patsy Hendren, was on board, along with Bill Edrich, Denis Compton and Godfrey Evans. Copious amounts of drink were taken and there was an almighty fracas between Fred Trueman and Edrich while they were stood by the emergency exit, puffing away like good 'uns (you could smoke everywhere in those days). Edrich had the temerity to suggest that Alan Moss was a better bowler than the man whose company he presently kept. Incensed, I think Fred tried to chuck him out of the emergency exit in retaliation.

Edrich did get off the plane sporting a black eye but that was from another incident, after he went and fell on a snoozing John Arlott. Awaking with a start that produced a reflex reaction of both arms shooting out, Arlott struck Edrich directly in the face. Undeterred, Edrich carried on tanking away when it came to the alcohol available and disembarked on Australian soil on crutches after he developed gout. It kind of devalued a theory I heard many years later from Ian Botham, that when you travel through as many time zones as you do to get from London to Sydney, you can drink as much as you want without it having an effect.

Also in our travelling party was Eddie Paynter, whose heroics of the 1932–33 series are forgotten because of the significance of England's Bodyline in the history of the game. After being hospitalised with a high fever and acute tonsillitis during the decisive fourth Test in Brisbane, Paynter listened to England's struggles on a radio before ordering a taxi to the ground and walking out to bat, to the astonishment of those there to witness one of international cricket's most talked-about series.

As I mentioned, it was Alec Bedser, the England tour manager, who had introduced me to Bradman in November 1974 when we had a day off. A small group of us, including the assistant manager A. C. Smith and our Australian scorer John Sands, better known to us by his nickname Shifting, went to see Think Big win the first of back-to-back Melbourne Cups.

Bedser would be all suited and booted in his position as manager as he would be received by dignitaries all over Australia. On one such occasion immediately following a bowl in the nets, which – in the absence of a tour tracksuit – he would complete in his vest, suit trousers and a nice pair of brogues. It seemed like the perfect attire for the conditions, not being so hot – only about 42 bloody degrees! He'd be stinking like a big Alsatian at the end of that but, once the beads had been reduced, he would shove his shirt, tie and jacket back on and sit with the important folk again.

He was so dressed when we bumped into Bradman on our way to the train. It was a great day among the punters. But I digress.

The memorable meeting with the Don came at the official gathering for the centenary match at the Melbourne Cricket Ground. We were effectively on an equal footing. I was a member of the touring entourage and all of Australia's ex-players were there, too.

All of us were included to make an extended team photograph taken at the ground, and they made a real fuss of all of us. Obviously, somebody like me was just making up the numbers but the inclusion of the old boys I have mentioned from the England side of the Ashes divide, plus people like Neil Harvey, Richie Benaud and all these fantastic cricketers dating back to the 1920s and '30s made it such a memorable event. We may have been treated equally but some were naturally more integral to the sense of occasion than others.

And the gathering of so many ex-Ashes stars in one location represented a fantastic opportunity to mark the occasion with memorabilia. And it was not only cricket fans who were collecting autographs. The majority of the players were struck by the sense of occasion and chased them, too, with the Don front and centre in everyone's targets. The kingpin of the signatures.

To me, this emphasised that whatever images people may

have developed of a player, however they project themselves to the public – and Bradman was not necessarily popular with his contemporaries or those he would go on to manage as an administrator – the very best are forgiven for their negative traits and revered for their ability. Everybody wanted him, and so the rest of us, with our accumulative total of hundreds of caps, were asked to form an orderly queue. That's when I got into conversation with the great man.

I happened to have taken the Stuart Surridge bat with which I scored a double hundred against India in 1974, and got him to sign that, among other things. I also had a number of miniature bats with me that I have locked away these past 30-odd years, signed by the great players. All these fantastic names have been preserved clearly and that is down to storage. As collectors will tell you, they must be packed away, distanced from sunlight, so that they don't fade.

This not-to-be-missed opportunity wasn't lost on Brian Close. He came prepared.

Now, I don't know how he had got them through excess luggage but I've never seen so many bats carried by a single player. Having been told to form an orderly queue, Brian would get a couple of things signed, then loop around again with a load more stuff. Very shrewd.

Bradman was very polite and patient in the circumstances. Inquisitive, too. When I got to the front, he broke the ice with: 'Is this a special bat, then?'

'It is actually. I got a double hundred with it against India.'

'Well done. I saw it!' he claimed.

You what? How the hell he would have done, I'll never

know. Perhaps he'd read about it. Perhaps he was aware of it and was just being kind. But I would like to think that the Don somehow did watch my career highlight at Edgbaston. Pity I never got a fifty against Australia.

I have got drawers full of miniature bats, but the Bradman autograph takes pride of place, and whenever I see it the first thing I tend to think about is Bodyline. For many an Englishman it will be the same.

He was obviously the greatest player we've ever seen. And I was able to relate those battles he had combating the short-pitched bowling of Harold Larwood with what I myself faced in 1974–75 against Dennis Lillee and Thomson, and the duel Derek Randall had in this landmark match. Randall's 174 was a brilliant innings in a memorable match, his defiant doffing of the cap to Lillee prior to being struck on the head by the Australian fast bowler its most famous image. Us ex-players feared England were going to get hammered but courtesy of a fine fightback, the eventual margin of defeat was just 45 runs, providing a wonderful symmetry. The first Test match back in Australia in the 19th century had been settled by the same margin.

During Bodyline, Douglas Jardine's England tried to reduce Bradman and they did by half, but he was still a great player. So natural. But one with an unorthodox technique. He had a backlift that went out to gully yet the bat still came in where it should be, nice and straight and through the line of the ball. Obviously, he must have been head and shoulders above everybody else even considering the great players that were around. England also possessed two all-time greats in

Wally Hammond and Len Hutton, but as good as they were, they could not get near the Don.

It had taken tactics of great controversy to curb this force of nature, but in a game driven by statistics his numbers were still exemplary by the standards of mere mortals. In what amounted to an ordinary series for Bradman, he still averaged 56.57 and his one hundred was also a skinny return.

So would he have thrived in more modern times when persistent short-pitched bowling was abundant? My view is that the very best of any generation adapt, and the speed with which he picked up length and the quickness of his feet in going forward or back would have been crucial. When you listen to him being interviewed on those old black and white television pictures, and he talks batsmanship in his very distinctive high-pitched Australian voice, you can just tell that he had an insatiable appetite for runs.

He must have worked so hard to counter the problems Douglas Jardine's England threw at him and would have worked even harder on the technical side had the need arisen. Watch footage of him in action and it reveals how decisive he is and how early he is in position for each particular stroke, especially for the pull. In interviews there was always a bit of Geoffrey Boycott in his responses. A declaration that nothing would stand in the way of being successful at the crease, and that he was going to work his nuts off to ensure that he did it. When people talk of him, they linger on the free-flowing sweep of the bat in the attacking strokes. Yet with one lapse in concentration none of it is possible.

Bradman's Test batting average of 99.94 is the most famous

statistic in the sport and arguably all sport. Only Steve Smith and Herbert Sutcliffe, of those to have played 25 Test matches or more, have averaged over 60. The gap between him and the rest is large enough to leave him indisputably top of cricket's batsmen.

In the 1930 Ashes, he contributed an astounding 974 runs in a five-match series. At the age of 21. Australia had unearthed a post-war national hero. No batsman in history has been so relied upon to contribute match-winning scores so frequently. His runs influenced results.

And he was an attractive player. A tight defence, yes, but Bradman still got on with it. The attacking nature of his play was one of the reasons they talked about Dougie Walters being the next Bradman in the 1970s. Walters operated in a very similar way, was totally natural as a stroke-maker and had people asking 'How does he do that?' But his problem was that he really could only play on home soil because when he went away and the ball moved around, he looked vulnerable. In contrast, Bradman played well all over the globe and did brilliantly in England. They were the same sort of busy, wristy dashers but the Don had the all-round game due to decisive defensive movements and quicksilver feet.

The thing that I believe links the best players throughout history is their wonderful hand–eye co-ordination. Bradman's was honed growing up in country New South Wales by hitting a golf ball or ping-pong ball with a stump against a corrugated water tank for hours on end out the back of his Shepherd Street family home in Bowral. That not only takes great discipline but forces the individual to cover the ball shooting off at unusual angles and producing erratic bounce, and because the 'bat and ball' are smaller, it centres the striking so that when bigger bats are introduced it feels easy.

Plenty of technically correct batsmen have super international careers but the ones in the very highest bracket, like Bradman, Steve Smith and Kevin Pietersen, have that hand–eye thing going on.

It means that even with imperfect techniques, everything is purposefully in sync when it comes to their movements. You can talk about the necessity of going back and across but that wasn't Sir Garfield Sobers. He stood still. Another in the highest tier, Graeme Pollock, worked from a wide stance. They have shown there's room for everything in terms of stance and trigger movements. It's their shared ability to react that provides the illusion of them possessing an extra second to play the ball.

Right now, the Don has company in the Steve. Steve Smith returned in mid-2019 from the year-long ban imposed upon him by Cricket Australia for his part in his country's ball-tampering scandal and was scoring runs for fun with a totally different technique to anybody else in memory. Smith's 774 runs in four Ashes Tests in 2019 was Bradmanesque. Whenever on commentary I always thought 'He's a big bastard is this bloke,' but then when you get stood next to him, he ain't that big. He's a six-footer, no KP at 6ft 4ins, and I think he gives the illusion of being bigger than he is because he is so imposing at the crease, with the way he blocks out the stumps with his trigger movements.

He's developed a technique that sees him go back and across as the bowler gets into delivery stride, and although it looks like he is in a totally inappropriate place, it's his hands and his eyes that get him where he needs to be. He's clearly worked it out for himself that the positioning of his feet is irrelevant as long as his head is still, rather than read it in anything, because that kind of approach just wouldn't be in any kind of coaching manual. He can end up in all kinds of improbable positions and still strike the ball cleanly from the middle of the bat.

He just doesn't miss and you can tell with Smith that teams are scratching their heads, thinking, 'How the hell do we get this bloke out?' Indeed, it was this that prompted me to come up with the idea of asking the general public that very question during Sky Sports' coverage of the 2019 series. On my tours around the various grounds, everyone I asked seemed to come up with the same answer: 'I have no idea.'

You can't teach what Smith has as a batsman, it's just him, and what that tells you is there's room for all sorts of methods and styles in the game – not least in bowling actions. India's Jasprit Bumrah, the Sri Lankan great Lasith Malinga, the South African left-arm wrist spinner Paul Adams: they're all different. Bumrah's braced bowling arm, Malinga's endangering umpires' ears, Adams, the man nicknamed the Frog in a Blender, looking at the floor as he delivered the ball. How do you teach any of that? You don't. You can either do it or you can't.

Smith faces competition for top rank from Virat Kohli, another fabulous player who has a different set-up again in terms of technique and approach to batting. He is driven to be the very best India has produced, and I think he's well on his way, courtesy of a fantastic defence that will get him over tricky periods. Once he does get over them, he has shown that he will go through the gears and that reaching a hundred is just the start. Graham Gooch used to talk about 'daddy' hundreds – so dubbed for being much bigger, and closer to 200 than just a round 100 – and Kohli is insatiable in the way he accumulates these.

I view him as a more conventional batsman, someone who's got all the shots and unlike Smith would feature in the text-books. He is viewed as a good attacking player, but I would argue he is more than that because he knows when to attack, when to move through the gears, and that puts a player on a higher pedestal. Flip this the other way round and consider someone like Jason Roy, who didn't survive in Test match cricket. Is his attacking play as effective as that of Kohli? Yes. So why did he not flourish? The answer is because he couldn't defend. His game is attack, attack, attack. It would have been interesting to me if the England selectors had given him 20 Test matches to see whether he could develop a technique. A box-office one-day player, exposed at Test match level because he just couldn't keep the good balls out.

Go back one generation and the best two batters on the planet were Brian Lara and Sachin Tendulkar. The way I would split them is by saying that Tendulkar was technique, technique, technique, while Lara was hand–eye co-ordination. While Tendulkar's ball striking was compact, the arc Lara created from up behind his head was huge. Again, he just looked different from the other leading players of his era.

There are echoes here of Bradman, who made such exaggerated sweeps of the bat when playing his strokes, and embraced his individuality to the full in his drive to be the best. Doing so became an obsession, to the point where he cut himself off from others.

Yes, the boy from Bowral was a world superstar but he was certainly not everybody's cup of tea. Travel around Australia these days and people will acknowledge his ability, but you get plenty who would say 'not a great bloke'.

Teammates described him as aloof. His post-match ritual on that astonishing tour of 1930 was to retire to his hotel room, write in his diary and listen to a phonograph, and his daytime achievements only served to emphasise the regard he was held in compared to the rest of the Australian team. Following his world-record Test score of 334 at Headingley, an Australian expat settled in the UK handed him a cheque for £1,000 as a token of his admiration. The rest of the players were irked that they were not offered a share. Not even a drink, in fact.

Adulation back home was disproportionate, too. Once back to Australia's west coast, he disembarked to attend welcome home functions alone and was showered with gifts from companies.

Between that series and the famous clashes with Douglas Jardine and co. in 1932–33, he also contemplated becoming a professional with my lifelong club, Accrington, in the Lancashire League, a proposal that was eventually warded off by a conglomerate of companies offering him employment, such as writing a newspaper column and talking on the radio, and remaining as an Australian international. He believed a cricketer should be allowed to maximise his earnings on and off the field.

Yet his personal crusade for better pay was not necessarily reflected in his dealings as an administrator in the 1970s when he perhaps treated the Australian Cricket Board's money as if it were his own during negotiations. He was very dictatorial. A real 'my way or the highway' kind of guy.

What made him one of the greatest characters of the game was his self-absorption. It was at the heart of his remarkable career statistics. He always backed himself over everyone else.

This ruthlessness might be required to get to the very top, whereas at the starting point of the game a greater generosity of spirit is required. Thankfully, my early experiences as a boy had people with this kind of quality in spades. Not so much 'What can people do for me?' as 'What can I do for you?' Those first few years of learning the trade, as Bradman did alone in his backyard, are what shapes you as a cricketer and I am grateful to some wonderful people for setting me on the right road.

CHAPTER 2

The League

All young players need encouragement. Cricket, after all, is a game full of pitfalls in which one mistake could cost you or your team dear. Things have a tendency to go wrong as you are feeling your way into the sport and, even when they are going well, it can sometimes feel like a disappointment not to have done better.

It was no different for me as I came through the ranks at Accrington Cricket Club, and my guiding light was a chap called Jack Collier, the first XI wicketkeeper. Jack had great empathy for lads who were trying to improve in what was a tough school. Believe me, playing first XI in the Lancashire League at the age of 15 in the early '60s was a chastening experience.

Forget schools cricket. In fact, don't get me going about it. When has cricket ever been played properly at schools? And I am not talking about the ones you pay thousands of pounds a term for. I mean state ones. Children are either taking exams or on their holidays. I never played cricket at school and neither did any of my four kids. It was down the club where you were taught the nuts and bolts of the game. A really vibrant place for learning.

Part of the attraction of hanging around Thorneyholme Road as a teenager was the number of overseas professionals that were employed. It was like a Hollywood A-list of cricket. Bobby Simpson, one of Australia's finest players, was followed by that great of the Caribbean, Wes Hall, and then Eddie Barlow, of South Africa, as Accrington's pro, and Ian Chappell and Charlie Griffith were recruited by Ramsbottom and Burnley respectively. I was not the only one hanging around collecting autographs.

Of course, being down at a cricket club encourages you to play cricket and I would spend hours honing my back-of-the-hand left-arm spin, and it caught the eyes of some of the club's hierarchy because every now and again while hanging out down there I'd get invited to go and bowl at the seniors in the nets. Alternatively, they might pop down on junior nights and ask: 'Could you come down and bowl at the seniors, lad?' It would make you feel 10ft tall.

Before long, the players I looked up to – the big-hitting captain Lindon Dewhurst, the Rushton brothers, Frank and Derek, Jackie Hope, Les Carter, Jim Eland, Eddie Robinson and Russ Cuddihy – were no longer just great influences during my formative years but men I would call teammates. They were in their twenties and thirties and I was still in short trousers, but they were willing to help with advice and support. Hall, the great West Indies fast bowler, also looked

after me, giving me a bat with a few miles left on the clock –
a Norman O'Neill Crockett, from Australia – when he was
ready for a new one.

That bat did me brilliantly, and after getting a bit better
each time I went to practice, and scoring some runs in the
second XI, they picked me for the first time in the summer of
1962. The following season I would be opening the batting.

It was a difficult relationship. The Lancashire League was
time cricket on pitches with little or no pace and so, although
bowlers struggled to get me out, I couldn't get any runs of
note. The upshot of this perpetual stalemate was that I used
to get barracked from start to finish.

There were certainly multiple times more 'get on with its'
than 'how's thats' when I was out there in the middle. The
most frustrating thing about this being that I knew all the
blokes who were shouting. It's not so bad getting an earful
from supporters of the other team. These people, though,
were the home spectators, and weren't very understanding of
my predicament. I was young, lacked the power of a grown
man and was up against some good bowlers.

Luckily, though, I had a guardian angel behind the stumps
in Jack Collier, a man who, when Wes was bowling, could be
found a darn sight nearer the boundary edge than the pitch.
In order to soften the blows to his hands when gathering the
thunderbolt deliveries from our great West Indies fast bowler,
he used to shove bits of steak into his wicketkeeping gloves.

He also used to pad the hits to my confidence with his
reassurances. Naturally enough, when I got out, I would
be disappointed and occasionally sat there with the odd tear

welling up because I'd not scored enough runs and been shouted at in the process of not scoring them. As I say, it was a tough school. The people that turned up and paid money to watch didn't go easy on young 'uns because of their tender years. The attitude was very much that if you were good enough to be picked in the team, you should be good enough to do the job.

Thankfully sometimes my misery would be interrupted by a massage as Jack would wander up behind me and give my shoulders a rub. The laconic delivery of words to go with it providing an even greater soothing element.

'Eee,' he would say. He used to start everything with 'eee' did Jack.

'Eee. You were going grand, lad. You were looking good today. I backed you for fifty.'

Bear in mind he would be saying this when I'd contributed about 10 runs to the cause, and taken up 15 overs doing so. He was just a lovely, lovely fella. The kind of experienced, enthusiastic, seasoned cricketer every club needs. One who puts the fortunes of the emerging generation above those of his own.

Jack, who passed down the family business to his grandson Sam Tucker, who is still keeping wicket for Church, had a great double act with another of our wonderful crew. Eddie Robinson bowled quick leg spin, although the majority of the deliveries that he fizzed down were googlies. At that time Lancashire had about four leg-spinners and he would have walked into any other county club's squad. Travelling beyond your own county boundaries for a first county contract somewhere was still a rarity at that time, though. So he would turn professional in league cricket instead, more than holding his own in the Northern League, his bowling complemented by the fact he could also smack it with the bat.

What a character. One of the funniest blokes I've ever played cricket with and someone I spent a lot of time with all year round as we played football together in winter for Cambridge Street Methodists, too. In fact, one of the things about the Accrington first XI is that most of us were footballers. Eddie was centre-forward and I was left-half. He was like lightning. That quick that all I would do was look to get him in behind the defence. He used to play off the centre-half in anticipation of this and if you struck a diagonal ball well enough they would never catch him.

He didn't like the cold, though, sometimes resorting to playing in a scarf and gloves, and on others deciding that not even the extra layers were enough. Take a game at Haslingden. Snow was underfoot, covering a frozen surface, and upon leaving the pitch at half-time, he declared: 'I'm not playing any more. I'm going back to club.' 'Club' being the working men's club. He'd scored a couple to be fair to him and true to his word he cleared off, clearly content that his work for that day had been done.

He was a bit of a law unto himself when it came to football due to the plunging temperatures of winter months, but you knew what you were getting with his bowling once the sun came out and he warmed up. His googly did for many a batsman. It also occasionally did for our Jack, too.

Stood up to the stumps, he was enthusiastic enough about

the pressure being exerted on the batsmen until one slipped down the leg-side for four byes. At that point, Jack would put his hands on his hips with his gloves and apologise. 'Eee, I'm sorry about that, Robbie. They're coming down like snakes. I'd given that up. I'd thowt it' bowled him.'

In any of the local pubs – The Crown, next to Accrington Stanley's ground, was *the* pub to go in – Eddie would hold court. He would have you in tears with the stuff he would come out with. Just everyday chat from what he had seen going about his week as an electrician.

Eddie provided the stories, Russ Cuddihy the steel. Russ has just gone 80 and coached cricket for years and years and years after hanging up his own boots. Great Harwood was the club that benefited from his passion for the game since retirement, while his daughter Victoria is now coaching women's cricket.

He had a reputation as a hard nut, a real tough guy, but beneath that exterior lay a heart of gold. Russ played professional football for Accrington Stanley and, as he lived really close to the base for our church football team, became a coup signing.

How to describe his attitude to football? Well, he'd eat people. As a half-back he would take no prisoners. You're talking about the early 1970s when it was normal for folk to be sliding in from behind to instructions from the referee like 'carry on' and 'ball first'. You would be half crippled playing Sunday League. There were plenty around like Russ on our patch, too. But he was a terrific sportsman.

As I was developing as a teenage cricketer with ambition,

it was blokes like these who were all willing me to do well. There was no nastiness at all, no jealousy, no selfishness. They were all full of encouragement. There would be shouts of 'go on, go on, keep going' when I batted. I felt backed. It's a fine thing when a sports team become great mates and in that regard I've never had so much fun. I've got this reputation as someone who likes a bit of a laugh and that's where it all started for me.

Some of the characters who were playing when I started were still turning out on a Saturday 20 years later when I returned as a professional after packing up with Lancashire.

In the 1950s, there was a notorious gang in London called the Richardsons, who would later be involved in turf wars with the Krays. Well, Accrington had their own Richardson clan. Neville Richardson was our opening bowler and would sometimes share the new ball with Wes Hall, bowling big booming outswingers. He once took a six-for in the ransacking of a Ramsbottom team, including Ian Chappell for 33.

I played more cricket with his younger brother Alan, though. Alan had a reputation for someone who bought trousers with long pockets. If you ever lost him, you knew it would be pointless looking for him at the bar. You no doubt know of an Alan or two yourself.

He would go to fairly extreme measures to avoid spending money, in fact. Not least one winter when, on a particularly cold night, he braved a blizzard to walk the three-quarters of a mile from his house to Burnley Road Bowling Club, where Russ Cuddihy was the steward. It was an establishment we all frequented. Loads of people we knew would socialise there, sitting out in the beer garden on the nicest summer days, or pop up for a game of snooker in winter.

On this occasion, though, Alan was on a mission through the snow. He neither wanted to sit in the beer garden nor play a frame or two. Instead, he walked into the club and asked Russ: 'Have you got a slice of lemon, please?'

'What for?'

'I'm afraid Cynthia's got a cold. And I want to put it in some hot water along with some honey.'

It was clearly no expense spared for Mrs Richardson either, from a man known around the club as Shitbag Richie. The nickname not a reflection on his behaviour, but by virtue of him working for a fertiliser company from Oswaldtwistle called GEM. In simple terms, he sold bags of shit.

Alan was a big, powerful lad, which was a good job after his decision one September to leave his cricket bat outside his back door for the winter. It had got into his head that it would be better letting the elements get to it. By the time he picked it back up the following April, however, it was like a railway sleeper. It had taken so much rain over six months that its edges had expanded drastically and it was twice the weight.

Like Richardson the younger, Brian Rutter batted a bit and bowled a bit. Another talented all-round sportsman. But he was one of those who was never happier than when he was miserable. I don't think I've ever seen him smile and I have known him for more than half a century. Enter a conversation with him and you lose the will to live.

You might recognise this prototype cricketer from your

own club. Bowls little swingers that are hard to get away and bats in the middle order and is always after a not out.

The Lancashire League threw up some great personal battles and I look back on some of them with great fondness. Jack Houldsworth was an opening bowler for Church. During the week he was an HMRC tax inspector but don't let his profession put you off. He was a great bloke. But for someone who chased pounds it was fitting that he could drop the ball on a penny.

Not much more than medium pace, but he was so accurate that you couldn't take any liberties against him. I recall being a sub pro for Nelson against Church in 1981. If for whatever reason a player wasn't required by Lancashire across a weekend, whether it was due to the fact you were coming back from injury or there was simply no game, you might get a request to deputise for the club's absent professional. The county provided the names of those available and the club in question would then choose the player they wanted. You would get a bob or two for turning out, a percentage of which went back to Lancashire.

So, here I was waiting to receive my first ball from Jack. He was at the end of his run with the ball in his hand and I knew what he was up to because he was noted in the league for his ability to raise the seam. There was no tougher bowler to combat when he did so either, because he hit it regularly and the ball would jag this way and that as a result. Whenever he did, you could hear the whirr of the thread no longer aligned with the rest of the stitching.

Detecting the sound as I negotiated that first ball, I took

guard again, this time about a metre down the pitch. I was going to play forward again because that's what you had to do on Lancashire League pitches against someone of Jack's pace. There were a couple of close catchers with me for company. Firstly, because it's the second over of the Nelson innings. Secondly, because I am already the villain of the piece being on deputy professional duty. Thirdly, I am from Accrington, and the rivalry with Church is massive. It all adds up to them being very keen to get me out.

Within a few deliveries, it was obvious that my front-foot lunge was making a right mess of the wet pitch. 'Come on, umpire, look what he's doing here!' The close fielders were on the case straight away.

'I tell you what,' I interjected. 'I'll come back into my crease as soon as he stops picking the seam.' Not that Jack ever would. For him it was just a way of life. What you did when you were brought on to bowl on a Saturday afternoon. As all the league's seamers worth their salt would. Jack finished with more than 1,100 career wickets and nobody ever clattered him. He was one of those bowling specialists. A cricketer that couldn't throw, couldn't field and was hopeless with the bat. But put a ball in his hand and he would be like a pudding pitch magician. He would bowl all day from one end with his little seamers from a nice measured run, getting in close to the umpire, and you just could not get at him.

It was a form of bowling that proved successful throughout the decades. A modern-day Jack called Dave Ormerod emerged at Bacup and then joined us at Accrington. Fondly known in the league by his nickname, Dibber. I've played against Dibber and thought that I would take him apart. Truth is I could do nothing of the sort. Operating at less than 75 mph, he was so accurate that every ball had to be played with a certain respect. If the pitch was rock hard and the ball was coming nicely onto the bat, then you would always fancy him going the distance but playing cricket in Lancashire meant the pitches never were like that. Bowlers like these guys would keep hitting the same area and by the end of the day there would just be a patch of soil left as all the grass had been knocked off.

Nelson's Pat Calderbank was very similar. In that match in 1981, I opened the bowling with Pat, who ran in about five paces. I ran in four. It was an economy of effort that went well rewarded. I took five for 57, contributed 15 with the bat, and we won by eight wickets. The game was finished about half past five and the club chairman was disproportionately delighted.

'Would you be available next time we need a pro?' he beamed.

'I don't see why not. Yeah,' I said. 'Although I am not sure I did that great.'

'Nah, it's nowt really to do with what you've done. The best bit is we've finished at teatime and the bar's full. If you get through them overs like that, you'll do for us.'

We had bowled 17 overs apiece in no time and apparently the bar takings had been brilliant.

Due to the proliferation of paceless pitches there didn't tend to be too many genuinely fast homegrown bowlers but Steve

'Dasher' Dearden, father of Leicestershire batsman Harry Dearden, was one. He took out Shane Warne's off stump on the Australian's home debut for Accrington in 1991 to bellows of 'send him home' – to Warnie, not Dasher – from some less sympathetic spectators at Thorneyholme Road. He was still sharp enough when I had one of my returns from retirement against Ramsbottom in 2008.

Players like him have made league cricket what it is. I can't speak highly enough of some of the dedicated players in the Lancashire League over the past 60 years. I am talking about some great club cricketers.

Bryan Knowles at Haslingden and Peter Wood at Rawtenstall both churned out thousands of runs. Bryan was once selected for Lancashire's second XI while Peter made two John Player League appearances for Nottinghamshire after coming to the attention of their captain Clive Rice. Similarly, Peter Brown at Burnley was a solid performer for many years. His two boys, Michael and David, both played county cricket. These were salt-of-the-earth, cricket-daft men, who exemplified the 'When Saturday Comes' competitive spirit.

There were friendships to be made everywhere. In fact, there was only ever one bloke with whom I kicked off. His name, rather aptly from a phonetical perspective, was Albert Ross. To me he was an albat-ross. I just couldn't shake him and he clearly affected me and my performances.

When I went back to play in the league in the 1980s, he gave me absolutely heaps. I was taken aback by it, too, because in county cricket I'd never had any bother. Yet now

I was being subjected to all kinds of abuse every time I came up against Todmorden. Real nasty stuff.

'Who do you think you are?' he would snarl at me. 'Big shot.'

I had not been used to owt like that, and more than anything at first it was the shock, even after I'd been warned: 'He's mouthy, this bloke.'

I didn't know him from Adam, but I couldn't get the question out of my head: 'What the hell's up with him?'

When I decided to give him some back, I was warned by his teammates: 'You want to be careful, mate, as he will nail you after the game.'

I thought: 'Oh, shit.'

Me and him had some real ding-dongs and it was the only relationship I had with anyone that was like that. I copped a bit from people when I came back to play in my sixties, and I was fair game then to be honest, given my age, but Albert was the first opponent who got stuck into me who was on my level.

In 19 years of professional cricket, and some international cricket during that time, I'd never been abused, never encountered such aggression. There was no one lurking with his kind of bile in county cricket. Even when I faced up to Australia in the 1974–75 Ashes, and the fast bowling beasts Dennis Lillee and Jeff Thomson, there was nothing.

I recall the home fixture at Thorneyholme Road in the summer of 1986, walking into bat at number six. We were 10 for four and he walked to the crease with me. Believe me, he wasn't offering me words of encouragement. It totally took me aback. I was out for nought, one of five ducks in an innings which featured a second-top score of five and we were dismissed for 48 on the way to a 10-wicket defeat. As Todmorden's opening batsman, Ross had a not out next to his name.

Later, I saw the funny side of it, accepted that it was just the way it was with him, and we actually got on great once we had packed up, but it took me a long time, and even now if I pop out to watch a bit of league cricket, I will get someone ask me: 'Seen much of Albert?'

Another stalwart was on the verge of breaking a record that has stood since the 1920s when the coronavirus pandemic decimated the start of the 2020 season. Keith Roscoe, a left-arm spinner, is an iconic cricketer in the league, who was 13 wickets shy of the number required to surpass Fred Duerr's amateur record of 1,811.

My name is among his vast collection of victims, although our playing days only coincided briefly in the 1980s when I had packed up on the county scene and he was building a reputation as a bowler of some note. He started his career with Bacup but has mainly played at Rawtenstall and that puts his efforts into some context.

Rawtenstall play on a postage stamp of a ground, with square boundaries no more than a 40-yard carry and that has meant Roscoe – nicknamed Kes as in kestrel because he used to hover around the older lads as a kid desperate to get a game of something or other – has had to come to accept getting 'pogoed' straight. To be fair, if you are making the batsmen hit to the longest part of a compact playing area, then you're giving yourself the best chance of them making a mistake – and lots have against him.

Funnily enough, he cites my lad Graham as one of the players who have made him suffer as a result of the ground's idiosyncratic dimensions, but as he says: 'I have been known to spin it! So if a batsman tries to smack it across the line, thinking that the shortest distance is up the terracing, and it does turn on them, they're gone. At Rawtenstall, batsmen can get away with murder, but they don't tend to keep getting away with murder.'

He is a bit of a personality. A spin-bowling punk rocker – the lead singer and rhythm guitarist in a covers band called Riflemen of War – he has dismissed some of the best players the league has had to offer. There weren't too many professional bowlers who dismissed the great Viv Richards twice in a season, but Roscoe got him three times in two innings as an amateur! The season was 1987 and, on two wet tracks, he feathered the outside and inside edges of the West Indies great's bat with his notorious arm ball. Wicketkeeper Peter Barnes held onto catches on both occasions and for the second match at Rishton had the wherewithal to remove the bails, too. The official dismissal went down as stumped.

Roscoe also snared Steve Waugh that summer and finished leading amateur wicket-taker in the league for the first of eight occasions. His performances earned a trial at Gloucestershire that July and August, and at Somerset the following year. Gloucestershire wanted him to uproot for Bristol but ties in the North-west, including a racing pigeon accessories business, a young son and a new mortgage, kept him on familiar territory.

'People say I have specialised in trying to get the best players out,' he says. 'But I tell them, "I've specialised in trying to get everybody out. I've just been lucky that some of them have been really good cricketers. I've got some really bad batsmen out as well!"'

Fewer players emerge onto the county scene from league cricket these days, but I was involved in pushing the cause of a cricketer who hails from one of the Lancashire League's best-known families.

As the club's barracker extraordinaire Big Roland, emerging from the bar when play was held up in the late 1980s, shouted: 'Who does that dog belong to? Get it off immediately, there's enough Barkers on the field already!'

There were three Barkers representing Enfield that afternoon: the father of Hampshire's Keith, Keith senior, and his two elder brothers, Gary and Andy. Fine cricketers all. Dad was a first-rate Lancashire League pro who did everything at the club: he was captain, coach, prepared the ground. You will no doubt have met lots of blokes like him at cricket clubs up and down the land. The ones that hold clubs and indeed leagues together with their devotion above and beyond the call of duty. Despite being born in Barbados, he played for British Guyana and his friendship with Clive Lloyd resulted in his youngest offspring, Keith junior, sharing the middle name 'Hubert' with the great ex-West Indies captain.

It was actually me that recommended Keith Barker to Warwickshire because he wasn't getting a look-in at Lancashire. My son Graham alerted me to him, saying what a thoroughly good player he was, and how he was 'too good for this league'.

It was 2008 and Ashley Giles was in his first year as director of cricket at Edgbaston and so I dropped him a note. Warwickshire despatched second XI coach Keith Piper to take a look at him, offered the chance of a trial and – when wickets and runs followed – a contract was on the table in the August.

Lancashire didn't like that I had recommended him. Earlier in his sporting career, he had chosen football over the contract they offered him and he was too talented to be sat on the sidelines waiting for another. I see nothing wrong with a lad trying to better himself and I felt duty-bound to help him get another chance. Those at Old Trafford had left it too late.

As things have turned out, he has had a lovely career. He played football at a good standard (he had Graeme Souness for a manager at Blackburn and made an appearance for England Under-19s) and then changed course when that door shut to enjoy a county cricket career of more than 250 appearances.

CHAPTER 3

The Barrackers

It is not only the friendships and associations that you develop with teammates and opponents that make being involved in the great game of cricket so appealing. Think of the weird and wonderful folk who make the games happen with their work around local clubs. They have nearly always got one or two screws loose. In a good way, of course.

Who in their right minds gives up their spare time free of charge to pitch in with the stuff that happens around the matches? Well, actually, some of the best folk I have ever dealt with, that's who. When I look back and remember the fun times, the laughs and those who have given me most pleasure, it is not only players who come to mind but those involved on the periphery.

Take Billy Ball, the announcer at Accrington Cricket Club throughout the 1980s, a period in which I had gone back to pro-ing in the Lancashire League following my retirement from the county scene. Radio Ball we used to call him. What a character.

He was the father-in-law of the opening bowler Ian 'Bertie' Birtwhistle, and lived within a stone's throw of our ground, Thorneyholme Road. This proximity proved useful if you were ever locked out of it because he was the one with the key.

As an announcer he was absolutely priceless and he used to have us all in stitches with his on-air demeanour and rapport with his audience.

At that time, we used to have a group of spectators that followed our matches. A bit like the lot that you regularly get gathered behind the goalposts at football matches. A bunch of die-hard supporters who cheered on the team both home and away. A very thirsty collective known as the Heavenly Choir. When they'd had a pint or two they used to make Billy's life hell – but they had a great sense of humour.

Billy loved the microphone but his confidence on it was put to the test every now and again when a visiting player's surname proved a challenge. His job was to announce the name of the new batter as they walked out to the middle but he hadn't a clue on any of the names, so you would often get the start of an announcement 'and the incoming . . .' followed by a lengthy pause. You would then hear him off microphone turn to somebody and ask: 'What's his name?' Or 'How you do you pronounce that?'

During this time, the league was becoming more ethnically diverse. Professionals like Mudassar Nazar, the Pakistan Test player, came from overseas, for example, and local lads with Indian or Pakistani heritage were becoming more involved.

Naturally enough, Billy's struggles with certain pronuncia-tions caused great mirth. Particularly when Lowerhouse were the away team. Lowerhouse were captained by the former Indian Test player Kirtivardhan Bhagwat Jha Azad.

After spluttering his way through Kirti's name, right on cue, the Heavenly Choir chimed up with their own version of the folk song 'Im Going Back To Himazas'.

'I'm going back to 'im Azad. 'Im as had a pub next door.'

Occasionally, Billy would get very serious, particularly if he thought the club was being short-changed. Accrington Cricket Club, to give you an idea of the ground and its environment, was located next to the public playing fields Highams, which has now been turned into a fabulous sports hub for the local community.

Now, if you went up on to Highams, which was higher than the cricket ground, it provided a perfect view for you to actually stand and watch matches. During this era, although we no longer drew the peak crowds of the 1950s, '60s and early '70s, you would still get a few hundred turn up and pay for the privilege of watching first XI club cricket. For the purposes of filling the kitty for the re-signing of a pro-fessional annually, this remained valuable weekly income.

As I say, the layout made for a perfect vantage point. However, it also exposed those who had dodged an entrance fee and Billy would be onto the skinflints in a flash. Even when the bowler was running up to bowl, sometimes in mid-delivery, he would bellow: 'Now then! To the gentleman stood up on Highams, we know you've not paid. Would you like to give a donation?'

Lovely bloke, Billy: never tired of his own voice and so he made the perfect announcer. He loved the microphone and his fear of it malfunctioning led him to test it regularly throughout a session of play. 'One-two, one-two.'

He completed more one-twos in a day than Franny Lee.

'Are we on? Are we on?'

To add to his performances, us players used to slip him notes from time to time. Any excuse to get on the airwaves, he was an absolute sucker.

The old classic was when he read out an urgent call for a Mr William Bailey to leave as his wife had phoned the clubhouse and required him immediately.

Within seconds the Heavenlies burst into song:

'Won't you come home, Billy Bailey,

'Won't you come home?

'She moans the whole day long.

'I'm gonna do the cookin' honey, I'm gonna pay the rent

'I know that I've done you wrong.'

Hearing the refrain of the early 20th-century song penned by jazz pianist Hughie Cannon, Billy was straight back at them: 'I know it's you lot down there setting me up, there's no need for that!'

All this while a game of Lancashire League cricket is going on as a backdrop to the Radio Ball show. He was absolutely priceless.

I was never sure where the Heavenly Choir got its name from, but they were a godsend when things got a bit stale on the field. A dozen of them followed us home and away and they were always up to some mischief or other. A very humorous bunch, one of them who went by the name Barbs used to come dressed in a vest and a top hat. His party piece, when things went a bit quiet, was to stand up and shout: 'Everybody that can't tap dance must be queer.'

All around the ground, folk would be having a go at it with him, even the players on the field. It looked like something out of *Riverdance*. To make things fair, he would give both the teams an opportunity to have a go by making sure he shouted it three to four times a game and at least once in each bowling innings.

He also demanded interaction with the team he was barracking for.

'Lloydy,' he would roar. 'Give us a thumb.'

My thumbs-up would coincide with a celebratory cry of 'Y-A-A-A-S' as if it was some significant juncture of the game. For that lot, I guess it was.

Of course, there's a parallel here to the Barmy Army in the sense that cricket is a social game to watch and crowds tend to like getting involved from the sidelines. The Heavenlies pre-dated the Barmies but the two groups clearly shared some common pastimes, namely having a good drink and a good singalong.

That connection between players and spectators has been developed over decades. From my experience in county cricket, most of the people who got involved in interaction from the stands tended to be sole traders, offering pearls of their own wisdom rather than singing in ensembles.

At Old Trafford, Draught Bass Harry was one of the best barrackers on the circuit. His party piece was to down a pint of Bass every time a wicket fell.

Then there was Big Head. Why was he known as Big Head, I suppose you are wondering? Well, it had something to do with his appearance. Flipping heck, this chap had the largest melon I have ever clapped eyes on.

Ken Dean, the name he went by to his mother, was a frightful sledger of players from the stands at Old Trafford, and got under the skin of the Lancashire players to the extent that both D. L. Lloyd (that's me) and the next generation of my family in G. D. Lloyd (that's my son Graham) were reprimanded by the club for going round during a game and threatening to fill him in.

Big Head's big bugbear was slow play and so he would be rather unsubtle about it should you err on the cautious side while batting. Both us Lloyds suffered at the hands of his wit.

Sometimes it would be a general request to 'Get on wi' it!' Alternatively, he would unleash one of his one-liners.

'Here, Lloyd, at least you'll never die of a stroke!'

Or 'Bowl him a piano, see if he can play that.'

On one occasion I snapped and sought him out. Perhaps I should have bitten my tongue, but I had just had enough and wasn't going to stand on ceremony any longer. He was going to get a piece of my mind. And he did.

The apple never falls far from the tree, I guess, and Graham's episode came during my three years as first-team coach at Old Trafford. I was oblivious to the fact that he had gone round to confront him but a couple of decades apart, both of us were reminded of our responsibilities when it came to conducting ourselves while on club duty. In the greater scheme of things it was no big deal. We were just letting off steam. There's only so much you can take and when you're struggling, the last thing you need is someone reminding you and the opposition of it with such slights.

Nigel Llong, now an elite umpire with the ICC, used to be a target for another Old Trafford regular, Norman the Postman, who sat in the members' end, which in the days before the square was rotated 90 degrees was side-on to the action.

Whenever he came out to bat for Kent, Norman would be waiting for him at the bottom of the pavilion steps, by the gate, with a very droll: 'Don't be Llong, Nigel.'

This gate in question, emblazoned with a red rose, was always operated by a steward in a white jacket but Norman would never be seated further than about three yards away and ready to put on his soliloquies whenever an incoming batsman from the visiting team was let through it and onto the field of play.

'No need to shut it, he'll be back soon,' Norman would chirp.

All fun stuff, of course, as long as you weren't on the receiving end of any of it. Being the butt of these kind of jokes went with the territory of being a professional cricketer in the 1970s and '80s but react and you risked being thought of as a killjoy or being hauled over the coals by the club's hierarchy. What made the barbs even worse was that the likes of Norman and Big Head had voices that projected far enough to be heard across the entire ground.

The smart Alecs weren't confined to the North-west,

either. Take Loppy Lugs at New Road, Worcester. He was a lovely, lovely old fella who looked like one of Snow White's Seven Dwarfs. He sported a shock of white hair and a stubby nose. And he used to play a trumpet all day long among the Worcestershire members.

Parp, parp, parp.

A 1970s version of Billy Cooper, the Barmy Army trumpeter, if you like. And as an away team you had to put up with it. Although for one particular Lancashire fixture, that didn't mean the duration of the full match.

The usual noise had been emanating from the old pavilion when a voice emerged in an interim of silence.

'Blow that thing once again and I'll snap it in half!'

Undeterred, Loppy Lugs continued.

True to his word, this chap confiscated the instrument in question and crunched it over his knee. He didn't quite manage to deliver his promise of leaving it in two bits but when poor Loppy tried to get another sound out of it, blowing like buggery, he couldn't. Not a peep.

Then, up the M5 at Edgbaston, Jim was the local entertainer. With his thick Brummie accent, he used to move around the ground shouting at individuals in a bid to gee them up. You could have all manner of career highs on your CV: England caps, Championship pennants, one-day titles. It didn't make you immune when it came to Jim.

He would be right on Willis's case, demanding: 'Come on, Bob, show us your England form.'

Or he would turn his attention to the opening batsmen John Jameson and Dennis Amiss at the start of the

Warwickshire innings, with encouragement that was straightforward enough, but rather incessant.

'Come on, Jamo,' he would cry.

When he'd had heard enough, Jamo used to shout back: 'Go and build another Fiesta, you daft sod.'

You see, Jim, who worked at the West Midlands car plants, was well known to the Warwickshire players. His heart was in the right place and, unfortunately from their perspective, so was his mouth, as intermingled with his individual encouragement was that of the collective variety.

'Come on, Warwick,' was a regular battle cry from whichever stand he had chosen to frequent for the particular session in question, and when things went quiet you could be assured that he was on manoeuvres to another part of the ground.

'I'm over here now, Warwick,' he would inform them, as if performing a duty akin to telling the umpire of the need to leave the field to change boots or pop to the loo.

Everybody around the dressing-room areas used to be pissing themselves at this bloke because there was nobody watching generally and he stuck out like a sore thumb. Or a foghorn.

There would be plenty of tactical advice, too. 'Put Eddie Hemmings on,' he would implore.

To his credit, though, he was not too proud to admit he was wrong or change his mind. When Eddie came on and got hit for four, he would demand: 'Take him off, take him off!' He was full-on all day was Jim. Non-stop, brilliant.

Another of his regular cries was: 'My mom says I'm daft.' To which, Jamo used to either mutter under his breath, or bellow back, depending on how his mood was: 'She's not f***ing wrong!'

With the Barmy Army, and individual songs of praise for players, times have moved on and you don't get players being so vocal in response as you used to. It used to be part and parcel of county cricket to have a two-way relationship. No matter how good you were, or how good you thought you were. Reputation was not an antidote to a severe dose of the verbals.

Back up in the North-west, Rawtenstall had a sledger-in-chief by the name of Jackie Barnes, who was revered around the Lancashire League for taking down the best with his wicked tongue. When it came to belittling the opposition, he was a bit like David aiming his sling at Goliath's forehead. The bigger the name, the harder they'd fall.

Woe betide you then if you were having a hard time of things. Every club used to have a professional in their first XI – even if injury-struck, league rules provided licence to sign a replacement – and if said player was bowling and subject to some stick from the batting side, he would launch into one of his verbal assaults.

'Which is pro? Put your pro on,' he would demand, straight-faced, in a shameless attempt to belittle the bloke who was being paid to be out there competing among the nine-to-five clubbies.

Two things were guaranteed about Jackie: whenever you saw him he would be wearing a flat cap, and he would make folk laugh with his off-the-wall comments.

Take Rawtenstall's club trip to Thwaites in Blackburn.

Yes, despite several claims they couldn't, they organised a piss-up in a brewery for their end-of-season social. So they all piled onto the bus, with number one supporter Jackie in tow.

During this beer tour, you start at the very top, the first stage of the production line, and follow it room to room. 'The brewing process starts by mixing malt with hot water to produce something called the mash. Liquid is then extracted from this, which we call the wort,' begins the guide, on a journey that feels as long as the fermentation.

They're all walking from one level to another to be shown how this filtering takes place, finishing with how the bottling and barrel plant operates once the beer is ready for its very final stages. They are shown how each bottle is filled to capacity and labelled. And also how barrels of beer are made up.

'And now, ladies and gentlemen, we can go and sample the beers in the sampling room.'

Of course, the majority of those present are not there for the education but the sup. So they're all gagging for a drink. 'Before that, any more questions you might have?' the guide asks.

To which, Jackie puts his hands up and says: 'When is it Blackburn holidays?'

It was the most random question that you could ever ask. Nothing to do with anything that'd been said throughout or the manufacture of beer.

While you would cock a deaf 'un to some of the comments from the stands, one person you had to listen to as a Lancashire cricketer was Bert Flack, the groundsman at

Old Trafford when I first joined Lancashire's playing staff in the 1960s.

He was an intimidating character. Let's just say that when it came to the running of the place, what he said went. Bert hailed from Norfolk but became Lancashire through and through, living onsite, which was important for a groundsman. Mrs Flack was in charge of all the cleaning so they were a good combination. He was the ground. She was house.

He was also in charge of security in an unofficial capacity. These days sports stadia are fully wired up with CCTV but back then there was a reliance on a much more primitive deterrent for trespassing in the form of Bert's dog, a ferocious Alsatian called Traff, as in Trafford.

Tardiness when getting showered and changed post-match came at a cost because if you left the dressing room late there was every chance that Traff would already be on patrol – and that meant a dash to your car during which you hoped to avoid being nipped on the arse or back of the leg by this snarling beast. Occasionally, you would slam the door behind you as its paws pressed up against the window. Forget pre-season tests, most of our lads did their best sprint times with Traff in pursuit of them.

This was also the dog that got hold of Tommy Drinkwater's pot arm after he somehow mislaid it on a visit to the toilet and come out with his jacket flapping about on one side.

'Where's your arm, Tommy?'

'Dunno. I had it when I went for a piss.'

Unable to find it, Tommy – a local league umpire who also

stood in second XI matches – eventually retrieved said limb but only after Traff had ragged it all around the car park.

Traff was an absolute menace and Bert indulged his ferocity by letting him loose whenever he got the chance, so if for example we were late coming home from away trips, having travelled in a certain number of cars, some lads would have to hop into their own vehicles upon return to Manchester. The arrangement was for us to telephone Bert en route and tell him the estimated time of arrival.

However, if it was after midnight, as it sometimes was, Bert would head off to bed and that would require us to scale the gates upon our return and knock on his front door to beg to be let out. All with Traff baring his teeth and snarling away.

Everybody in the game knew Bert and he didn't take any shit from any opposition captain. He didn't take shit from anybody, to be honest. In fact, should someone challenge him, he would get stuck right into them. There was no question that he ruled the roost at Old Trafford.

Take the tour match against Pakistan at Old Trafford in August 1974. It's a three-day game; I'm captain.

Now, it was universally accepted in a three-day game that if you hadn't been dismissed with half an hour remaining on day one, it was time to declare and subject the opposition to a concentrated period of pressure against the new ball. That's just always how it was.

Only Pakistan clearly hadn't read the memo. They batted on the first day, which admittedly featured reduced playing time due to wet weather, the second morning and at lunchtime they came out again with the intention of carrying on.

The game is already gone as a contest because of this attitude and they're clearly just using the remainder of the fixture as batting practice rather than high-intensity cricket to prepare for the Test matches.

Until the start of the afternoon session on day two when, as I am leading the Lancashire team back into the field, Bert is coming past us with the heavy roller.

'What's going on? We have not declared,' said Wasim Raja, as he made his way onto the turf.

'Well, you have now!' Bert informed him, and with that he started rolling the pitch.

He would often come and sit with us in the dressing room, and we thought nothing of it as he had been around that long he could be mistaken for a piece of the furniture. He also formed strong relationships with opposition players, and took a particular shine to Dilip Doshi, the Indian slow left-arm Test spinner who spent multiple years playing county cricket for Nottinghamshire and Warwickshire, calling him Dobie Dishwasher, a reference to the scouring pads used to do the dishes at that time rather than any electrical machinery.

As a captain of Lancashire, I was very fond of him, too, but the working relationship was an interesting one. My job was to ready the team; his to ready the playing area. Now, if ever I had gone to him and asked him for a just-so pitch, I would've got exactly the opposite. You got what you were given, and it was best to just leave him. He was an old-fashioned groundsman who would say, 'It's my ground.' And that's a tradition he has passed down to Pete Marron, then through to Andy Fogarty and Matt Merchant.

Between them they have prepared the wickets of Old Trafford for about 50 years.

Bert would mobilise a mopping-up team whenever the square suffered a drenching: as second XI players in the 1960s we would be drafted in to lay out enormous blankets, which would suck up the excess water like paper towels and when fully soaked required wringing out.

At this point, the junior professionals chosen to pitch in would be feeding them into Bert's manual mangle until they dried out and the buckets below were full, and then be expected to relay them and start the process again. Imagine asking Jimmy Anderson to work the mangle.

While Bert left team affairs to the experts, the same could not be said of the much-loved Ron Spriggs, the Old Trafford dressing-room attendant when I was first-team coach at the club.

I would always get in at 7.30 in the morning and head to the office that the then groundsman Pete Marron had created for me by converting the toilet block at the back of the pavilion, with a boarding up of the urinals, and the introduction of a desk and a phone.

If any of the lads had been a bit naughty, I would pull them in there but on a run-of-the-mill day it was the place for a breakfast cuppa and a bacon sandwich. Spriggo, Pete and I would all take a seat and tuck in.

'Who've you got your eye on, then? I tell you who you want to pick. I watched thingy-me-bob in the twos last week and he is better than any of them that you're going to stick in the first team.'

That sort of thing.

Dressing-room attendant he might have been, but he tried to pick the team for me! When we had someone out because of injury, or more likely on England duty, as was often the case with a squad that featured Michael Atherton, Jason Gallian, John Crawley, Neil Fairbrother, Mike Watkinson and Peter Martin, it meant a lad from the seconds needed to be promoted. The likes of Stephen Titchard and Nick Speak came in and generally did all right.

'Told you, told you, that were my shout,' Ron would insist, if they contributed a score.

At least Ron was only ever interested in putting a team sheet up on the wall, rather than a member of the opposing team as happened while his predecessor Jimmy Erskine looked after the players.

Jimmy had been acquired by Clive Lloyd, who was doing a bit of social work when he first moved to Manchester in the 1970s. Let's say Jimmy hailed from the rough side of Manchester, had been down on his luck and needed some help. Clive provided it by recommending him for the job of dressing-room attendant.

When Sussex visited, their overseas player Javed Miandad, of Pakistan, asked Jimmy to go and get Clive Lloyd's autograph on a bat. So Jimmy left the away dressing room and came upstairs to us, got it signed just so and toddles off back down.

'That's not Clive Lloyd's autograph,' Javed declared incredulously.

Jimmy's response was to grab said Pakistan superstar batsman by the collar and ram him up against the wall.

'You calling me a liar?'

Not a bloke you wanted to upset, he had to be dragged off and calmed down with a cup of tea in our dressing room. After an episode like this, you might have thought Javed would've learnt his lesson. As you will discover later, however, he did not.

Normally the threat of physical injury comes when someone steps up from their weekend club matches believing they can take on the professionals, as was the case when Piers Morgan wanted to show he was a Pom with heart during the 2013–14 Ashes. Irked by the way things were going for the England team against Australia, he was critical of the players and clambered on his high horse and said, 'Anybody can show some guts and determination,' in response to repeated capitulations at the hands of Mitchell Johnson.

Now everybody can form their own opinions about Morgan, and they will have done, no doubt, but I was there when it all kicked off with Brett Lee in Melbourne. I was working for Channel Nine as well as Sky Sports during that series, and after England relinquished the Ashes at the earliest opportunity in Perth before Christmas, Lee was very quick to take up the challenge of being the fast bowler to check the Morgan theory out.

The gauntlet was thrown down at teatime on the first day of the Boxing Day Test and the challenge was on. Sky agonised as to whether they should cover it but because it was considered that a serious injury could be incurred, they decided against it. Channel Nine, the host broadcaster, did cover it, partly because of the profile of those involved.

Morgan had become big news all around the world with his *Piers Morgan Live* television series in the United States and Mark Nicholas introduced him as 'the most watched chat show host in the world' as viewers were able to watch one of the most cricket-crazy men I have ever known kitted out in his gladiatorial gear. It was like the Colosseum with all these people baying for blood. The nets at the MCG are cut into the walkway to the ground which means that spectators can stand above and look down if someone is practising.

Brett Lee was absolutely fired up for this one-on-one for some reason, and we're talking about one of the fastest bowlers there has ever been here. He was still looking lean and decidedly mean. Piers, meanwhile, was stood awaiting cricket's version of a coconut shy with his shirt hanging out. He looked totally dishevelled. Probably due to the fact that one of the warm-up bowlers he had been facing in preparation had knocked him off his feet.

Despite that strike on the back of the head, however, when asked if he was feeling a bit nervous, Morgan played up to the showman image, replying, 'No, I think he's a bit nervous,' gesturing towards Lee with his glove-covered right hand.

'I see the Australians have come out to see a Pom with some real guts and spirit,' he added, referring to the hordes who had gathered up above him, 'and once I have dealt with Lee, I will be moving on to Mr Johnson,' pointing to a bowler who had been touching the speed of light during a series in which he took 37 wickets at a cost of under 14 runs each.

'I am going to do this for my country, to prove that we are not all quitters, and fight fire with fire.'

The sight of a bloke standing at the crease in an England shirt certainly seemed to get Lee's competitive juices flowing and a crowd wondering what kind of speeds the Australian could crank up from a medium-to-long run were not left wondering long.

First ball, Piers gave himself room and advanced, leaving his stumps exposed. Not that the bowler appeared to have bits of wood as his intended target, following the batsmen instead and thudding a short ball into his stomach.

'Didn't feel a thing,' Piers insisted.

The second one flew at just over head height, causing Piers to take evasive action and tumble backwards into the netting.

'Bring it on, mate, bring it on.'

Then some advice for his adversary: 'Try pitching one in my half!'

Blows to the hand and rump followed, Nicholas's offer of medical attention declined on each occasion and the wounds inflicted were not only those of pride. Lee's fifth ball bowled him neck and crop, removing leg stump.

'He's a bit quicker than I thought he'd be for his age,' Morgan conceded.

Flippin' heck. Brett Lee is one of the fastest bowlers that there has ever been and he was steaming in, and going through the crease, as all quick men will do if there's no umpire there to stop them. So he was actually bowling off about 19 yards – rapid. No wonder Piers was moving to the leg-side or as he might say 'giving himself a bit of room'.

Unfortunately, though, wherever he went, Lee followed. Fast bowlers know exactly where a batsman of limited competence is going, hence the ball kept rattling into his body.

What this mauling showed was that no matter how good a club player you are – and I am not convinced on the evidence presented that the bloke holding the bat on this occasion was one, sorry Piers – the massive difference is that you are talking about a completely different level in terms of the pace you are used to facing.

If he had had a go against Paul Collingwood he would have survived but let's recap the facts: this was Brett Lee, one of the fastest there has ever been, off 19 yards on a quick practice pitch at the MCG.

This whole episode reminded me of an interview between Jonathan Agnew and Geoffrey Boycott that was done late at night in the aftermath of England getting nailed by Johnson in Adelaide on what was a placid pitch.

Aggers is just shuffling some papers on his desk and says to Boycs: 'Well, England have been humiliated there by Mitchell Johnson and on such a placid pitch. It's not a quick pitch at all. How do you think you would have got on, Geoffrey?'

'How would I have got on with that pitch, against Mitchell Johnson? He'd have been bowling at me for a fortnight. And when I'd done with him he would have been like a midget.'

Midgets, I believe, rang up the Beeb to complain.

That night, as coincidence would have it, both myself and Piers had been invited to a party at Shane Warne's house in a Melbourne suburb called Brighton, and after chatting with Warney's dad, Keith, over a mutual appreciation of beer and pubs, I got into the company of Piers, who I'd never met before.

I told him: 'I watched that today and I was fearing for you.'

'Don't,' he said, with a self-deprecating smile. 'I'm aching from top to toe. I'm nursing two broken ribs and a broken thumb.'

'Christ!'

'I just couldn't show pain.'

So 10 out of 10 for effort, bravery and foolhardiness. At least he can say he's done it. They said he could have really got hurt doing that. To be fair, he did it, laughed at himself and as a result really went up in my estimation.

As an Aussie might say, 'Good on ya'. He had a go. Yes, he was totally out of his depth and in that sense it would be like somebody saying to me – and I've never, ever skied – put these things here on and get down that black slope. There's absolutely no way – because I know I am going to break my leg.

I've watched his career with great interest since and he just eats people for breakfast on *Good Morning Britain*. He doesn't let them get a word in edgeways if he knows that they're wrong 'uns and I reckon he goes out of his way to get wrong 'uns on his programmes. He nails them, absolutely nails them, should they be even slightly economical with the truth. So I have come to admire him for that.

The threat of physical injury is not restricted to the action either when you invite wannabe cricketers to play against the full-timers. I recall when I got asked to participate at a benefit day for Allan Lamb at the lovely little ground of Tring.

A two-leg event that started with a match, for which I was an umpire, and was followed by a dinner that evening at a pub next to Putney Bridge, for which I was guest speaker. There was a right cast of celebrities in their whites. There was Bill Wyman, bass guitarist of The Rolling Stones, and Andy Fairweather Low from Amen Corner plus Bungalow Bill Wiggins, who was keeping company with Joan Collins at this time. Naturally, he was the envy of the two dozen blokes gathered for this match.

Anyway, as I said, it was a benefit match. Or at least it was a benefit match to everyone apart from Bill Wyman. No: to him this was serious, and he and Andy Fairweather Low were in the nets knocking up for a good half-hour before play.

Not that it did a great deal of good. Opening the batting, Bill was out in the first over. Undeterred, though, he went straight back to the nets for more practice. The only mark either of them left on the game was at first slip at either end of the ground. That is where they had gathered for a chat throughout their team's bowling innings and by the end of the match there were two piles of fag ends.

The most rock 'n' roll they got, though, was after dinner was over when bets were placed around midnight on who had the nerve to walk the outer gantry of Putney Bridge. It might not surprise you to learn that Lamb was one. Or that another was a certain David Gower – he of the Tiger Moth flying squad escapade during the 1990–91 Ashes in Australia. Pulling stunts appear to have been a lifelong habit for that lad.

Cricket has a healthy following from the world of entertainment. Elton John was a regular visitor to England dressing rooms in the 1980s and famously sent a crate of champagne for the post-series celebrations during the 1986–87 Ashes.

And I have often wandered into the commentary boxes and been forced to double-take. Once I stumbled upon a bearded bloke doing the crossword. 'Who the hell's that?' I thought. It was only Eric Clapton. Then Mick Jagger turned up the following week. These days, I make sure I get selfies with the likes of Ed Sheeran.

Back in the day at Lancashire, a chap called Vince Miller, whose son Danny Miller is a fabulous actor in *Emmerdale*, was the compère of clubs in the Manchester area and he was cricket daft. He was very friendly with Clive Lloyd and so he would spend more time in our dressing room than some of our players. He'd turn up with acts who were booked for the week at the Poco Poco nightclub in Stockport like Roger Whittaker or Matt Monroe.

Music was clearly a big thing for us in the 1970s when we enjoyed our one-day heyday because, like football clubs used to, we made a record when we got to Lord's. Derek Hilton, a local musician, penned the words of 'We Will Always Stick Together', a single so popular that all seven copies flew off the shelf.

We turned up at Stockport's Strawberry Studios, where Joy Division, The Smiths and The Stone Roses all recorded, and I recognised the mixing engineer, who is flicking these sliders up and down, straight away.

'I know you,' I say 'You used to be in Wayne Fontana and the Mindbenders.'

'I did. Yeah. That's me.'

'You still playing?'

'I am, but I'm with 10cc now,' he says. It was Eric Stewart. He owned the place.

Farokh Engineer was in the team but he wasn't a very good singer and hadn't turned up for the official photo so we slipped in another of our mates, a comedian called Johnnie Goon Tweed – whose act used to be a take-off of The Goons – 'there is a tap on the door', 'funny place to put a tap' – into his place. There was more than a passing resemblance to our Indian star and so we stuck him in the middle for a laugh.

CHAPTER 4

The Red Rose

A county dressing room effectively becomes your home for half the year, and, if you are lucky enough to make a career out of the game, a good chunk of your adult life. Naturally enough in a competitive environment, you do not get to choose your housemates and so I am lucky to be able to say that I formed some great friendships in the 19 years I was on the playing staff with Lancashire. Ditto half a dozen more subsequently as a coach.

When I was taken on for the 1965 season, the funniest bloke with whom I played professional cricket awaited. Others have made greater impressions on me from a performance perspective, but none have provided more entertainment, and in a team that had more downs than ups when I first joined, the laughter he produced was an important factor.

David Green was quick-witted, always had a put-down if you chirped at him that was 10 times more amusing than the original wisecrack and was someone who would talk incessantly about inane things that would leave you in stitches. To him life was like one long commentary.

He would start from the moment we began our pre-season running drills on the outfield at Old Trafford. This would be done in groups and that meant some would be out on the grass while others sat and observed from a vantage point provided by two rows of cinema seats in front of the pavilion. We'd be sat there as if watching the latest film release. Greeny, as was his wont, provided the voiceover, which was more or less an analysis of the running styles of our colleagues. When the matches began, his critiques stretched to those of our opponents.

'Look at him, he's running like a galloping knitting needle,' he would say.

'Look at that bloke there. He moves like Harrison Dillard.'

Not such a bad compliment one would think, Harrison 'Bones' Dillard being an American Olympic runner. The only man ever to win both the 100 metres and 110 metres hurdle gold medals. The fastest sprinter in the world in 1948 became the fastest hurdler four years later. This man was the supreme athlete of his era.

But Green's comparisons were nothing to do with what may have been housed in the trophy cabinet. No, it was all about his attire and appearance. Dillard's shorts used to be pulled so high that they would disappear up his bum. He was a real Harry High Pants.

Referencing sports competitors from other fields and different eras was a running theme within Green's daily routines. After a post-match shower, he would stagger back into the dressing room, with his Y-fronts pulled up to his tits, and adopting a boxer's stance, would announce himself: 'Ace Hudkins, the Nebraska Wild Cat.'

There was no Internet, of course, so you'd have to remember who he had claimed to be that week and do your best to research them.

Ace Hudkins was a ferocious boxer during the 1920s who was never knocked out and whose fight against Sammy Baker was dubbed the bloodiest on record. He would mimic these blokes as if we all should pick up on their mannerisms.

To us, Green was like a walking encyclopaedia. His knowledge was impressive for a bloke who spent so much time in county cricket dressing rooms. He seemed to know everything, something the fact that he would complete the *Daily Telegraph* crossword within the hour only enhanced to an impressionable teenager. He was unbelievably clever. Then again, he was an Oxford University graduate.

There was not much doubting he was one of a kind among the Lancashire playing staff. You only had to see him turn up for matches to recognise that. Everybody else had cricket cases of varying sorts. I would think most people remember those leather ones which featured a side pouch to store your bat in that left the handles sticking out. The hard-cased coffin was another popular style.

Green used neither of these. He transported his kit in a suitcase. A proper, traditional suitcase that he would pop open the clips on every April. Whatever was revealed to be inside had been there since the previous September when he had placed it in hibernation for the winter. Out would come pairs of trousers like concertinas, fold upon fold, and crumpled old socks.

We did a lot of fitness during the month of April that represented our pre-season. We reported for duty on the first – when you look at the County Championship now, it is in full swing by mid-April and has been known to start in some years as early as the fifth of the month – to be put through our paces by Jack Crompton, who was Manchester United's former goalkeeper and had become fitness trainer at the other Old Trafford.

Alternatively, an Olympic sprinter called Barry Kelly would be in charge of getting us fit for the start of the season. There would be lots of running and agility work but there were no resistance bands or kettlebells in sight. However, like the class of 2020, we would finish up with a game of football on the back field. These days that back field is a car park, but it used to be a really magnificent square expanse of grass for our old 'uns versus young 'uns encounters.

There were a few of us who were more than decent players, good semi-pro footballers, but Greeny was a rugby player of decent standing, representing Sale in the winters once his suitcase was packed away. So to even things up when we played football, he would grab somebody from the opposition and sit on them. Literally rendering them unable to move. Believe me, he was a big bloke so if you were his chosen prey you were out of the game until he opted to move. There was no throwing him off.

So what of him as a cricketer? Well, he was pretty full on – a real dasher with the bat in hand who also bowled a bit of filthy medium pace. He ended up moving to Gloucestershire, and was followed there by Geoff Pullar 12 months later, after a bit of an issue with authority. Generally, he had not a care in the world. He was a professional but an amateur in his outlook, someone who just loved playing. To him cricket was a lot of fun while he hated the committee, which he termed 'that lot of the sharp end'. A phrase that he delivered dipped in sarcasm.

An idiosyncrasy of his was that he always wanted to get off the mark first ball, reasoning that the bowlers would be as stiff as boards and so if he couldn't hit their loosener for four then what chance would he have later on. So every now and again, to try to shift the balance even more firmly in his favour, he'd charge down the pitch to the first ball of the innings and have a burst at it.

He scored 2,037 runs in the 1965 first-class season, my first with Lancashire, without scoring a single hundred. The other two batters to get to 2,000 that summer, Colin Cowdrey and John Edrich, hit five and eight respectively. Nobody could match his haul of 1,784 in competitive matches (i.e. those in the County Championship).

He also breached the 2,000 mark in his first season at Gloucestershire in 1968, form that had him touted as an England opener and resulted in him being named as one of *Wisden*'s five cricketers of the year in 1969.

In between the two bountiful years, he had been on jankers at Old Trafford, which meant he was asked to captain the twos for a period during 1967. Captains generally set the tone on a behavioural level and the team culture under him was raucous to say the least.

In one particular second XI fixture, we were playing a Minor Counties Championship match at Millom against Cumberland, staying at a pub with rooms, as was often the case for away trips. We were quite a young group and, always keen for some mischief, Greeny summoned us to the bar for a team meeting. It was a ruse to socialise.

He locked the door with explicit instructions that nobody was to go to bed. The drink of choice (although certainly not mine during a stage of my life in which half a lager and lime was about as heavy as it got) was Parfait d'Amour, which for the uninitiated is a bright purple liqueur that tastes like paraffin.

Eventually, in the wee small hours he let us get to bed and next morning rocked up to open the batting. Our opponents had a captain called Harold Millican, who it was rumoured had a metal leg, and Greeny made it his goal in that innings to hit it. Millican was stood at mid-off, and despite being the target for a clang or two, had the last laugh when he intercepted one of the drives aimed at him, catching Green for nought.

I got stuck in at number three, scoring 54, which meant I got sent down to play for the first team against Middlesex in Manchester immediately after what turned out to be a drawn two-day match was concluded. Most of my teammates would have wondered how I managed to perform so well after the liqueur night, but I can reveal that I simply chucked my drinks in the plants that adorned the room whenever no one was looking.

Green departed at the end of the season, but his sense of

adventure stuck with me. Later in life, he became a *Daily Telegraph* cricket reporter. These reports were very bland compared to the colourful character known to us and Gloucestershire, where he played for three years before retiring for journalism at the age of 34.

Another left-hander in Geoff Pullar looked after me from a batting perspective in those early years on the Lancashire playing staff. Pullar, who was converted from a middle-order batsman to opener by England in the late 1950s and averaged in excess of 43 in his four years in the national team, took me under his wing, ignoring the fact that I was going to take his job. It didn't make any difference to him, and that showed him to be a real team player.

He was always good with advice, telling me how to play in different conditions and against different bowlers. For example, when we came up against Fred Trueman in Roses clashes, he would remind me 'just get forward. Play forward.' On uncovered pitches, Trueman wanted you to play back because he would be pitching it up, allowing the ball greater distance to misbehave and leaving you with little reaction time.

Pullar also taught me about cutting: that it is always about the length of the ball when deciding whether or not to play the stroke, because you can always make room, and if it lands right and your hands are good, you can play it late. And how to play spin: use your feet.

After I got none and none in my debut against Fred Titmus and Middlesex in mid-1965, I was unbelievably disappointed. That kind of return zaps a young player's confidence. Geoff knew that and was waiting with advice in the nets over the next few days.

'Where did you think you could score?' he asked me.

'I couldn't see any runs,' I told him.

'Well, you have got to try to get down the pitch in that scenario,' he continued. 'Try to disrupt him, make him think of something different. You have got to have confidence.'

He added: 'When you come down to meet the ball, make sure if you miss it, it hits you, don't come the wrong side of it and let it slide past the edge of your bat.' Geoff would always look to play the ball leg-side, and exaggerated that by getting offside of the ball. These snippets of information were effectively my coaching.

Experienced players like him would be giving you information that you could apply to your own game. At practice sessions, there's a fair amount of standing around in which you tend to get chats going with other players who have experience of similar scenarios.

There were coaches to talk to as well, although they were not akin to the modern tracksuit variety. Take Stan Worthington, whose 11 years in the position of coach with Lancashire officially finished in 1962, the summer before I began my apprenticeship at Old Trafford. Instead of training gear, Mr Worthington – a legendary figure at the club – would be decked out in formal wear. His trademark attire comprising trilby, cravat and cigarette holder. Quite a dapper chap.

Things were very formal in his regime, including the running of regular trial days at Old Trafford. By the way, as far as I am aware Lancashire are yet to ever take anybody onto the playing staff that originally came to the attention of the club through a trial. It's an extraordinary statistic.

But Worthington tended to receive letters from people asking to be given the chance to show what they had to offer, and so all this correspondence would be pooled together and the individuals in question invited to specialist training days at the start of each season.

Some of these wannabe Washbrooks and maybe MacLarens were clearly delusional. Some were just coming down to have a bit of a hit even though they were hopeless. One lad who turned up looked like he needed a good feed, and so he was in the right place because the one thing the club guaranteed to anyone who turned up was a free lunch in the players' dining room.

Although a cricket coach is customarily visualised in the nets, this truly was Worthington's domain. The dining room was where he would provide lessons on etiquette. Things like how to stir a cup of tea properly. He didn't like a cricket team to look like a group of unruly youths. It certainly wouldn't have sat well with his debonair image.

Anyway, Hungry Horace, the lad in question, had bowled a load of shit in the nets. It's never easy bowling on an empty stomach, I guess. But he seemed to gain a spring in his stride as he marched to the serving hatch to take one of the mixed grills, and his place opposite Stan. Without further ado, he launched his fork, stabbed a grilled tomato and shoved the whole thing into his mouth, not giving any thought to the fact that it would be red hot. As a reflex, he spat it straight out, and it landed 'boom' straight on Stan's forehead.

The place was in uproar. Stan was apoplectic. And that lad never did get the chance to bowl in the Old Trafford nets again.

Stan was unbelievably strict and liked to impose his particular rules and regulations. He didn't readily accept anything that was outside what was accepted behaviour in society at that time.

For example, we had John Sullivan and Harry Pilling, two salt-of-the-earth guys who played cricket by day and dashed off to gigs at night. They were in a harmony group that put on shows at local pubs and were running late one evening after an extended day's play, so instead of waiting for showers to come free jumped in the bath together.

Stan happened to open the door at an inopportune moment to witness them and arrived at the wrong conclusion. 'If I catch you doing this again, you will be straight out of the door,' he warned, clearly in the belief that the two were getting a little bit too harmonious. That sort of thing was taboo in the early 1960s.

He had spent his playing days at Derbyshire, where he was a member of the 1936 Championship-winning team, the only Championship-winning team in the club's history, and he also won nine England caps in an extraordinary career. He began first-class life as a number 11 but scored a Test hundred and played as an opening batsman in an away Ashes Test.

The players knew that Stan had pedigree but, boys being boys, it did not spare him the odd prank. They used to say that he would turn up unannounced to watch second XI matches or net sessions, but any chance of doing so incognito was habitually dashed by the omnipresent trilby protruding from his head. It had been the case for a Minor Counties Championship fixture away at Northumberland when all concerned were staying at the same guest house. Said hat had been left on a stand in the reception area, and thus became the perfect ball in an impromptu game of rugby when a group of players returned from the pub one evening.

By the time it had been drop-kicked up and down the hall it bore a greater resemblance to a rag than a hat.

Those players were to witness its state at breakfast the following morning when Worthington, a fearsome individual when roused, ventured into the dining room, held it up and said: 'I believe there was a game of rugby in the hallway last evening, featuring this. Tonight, you will have another opportunity to play. Only this time, my head will be underneath it.'

Worthington's successor was a chap called Charlie Hallows, whose claim to fame as a stylish left-handed batsman was to score 1,000 runs in the calendar month of May. Traditionally, it used to be that the leading batsmen in the country would target reaching four figures by the end of May and therefore modern attempts have included runs scored in April. Back in 1928, however, the season began on 2 May, putting Hallows in revered company. The only other two men before him to have made the thousand exclusively in that particular month were W. G. Grace and Wally Hammond. No one has managed it since.

I am not sure a bunch of upstart young cricketers fully appreciated his status when he was headhunted from

Worcestershire. He belonged to a completely different world to us, being in his late sixties. He would be 74 years of age when he gave up the post.

During those seven years, my overriding memory of him and his coaching advice came at a Championship game against Kent in Blackpool in the summer of 1966. I was batting at number eight. We were batting first on an uncovered pitch and so, as a player in his first full season as a first-team player, I asked him: 'Charlie, what do you reckon? What should I do here, coach?'

To set the scene, the Kent seamers David Sayer and John Graham had had a go on the Stanley Park pitch, and the former had bagged a couple of early wickets in the shape of David Green and Jack Bond, when Colin Cowdrey, the visiting captain, brought Derek Underwood on just to have a look at what might happen.

What happened might be termed minor carnage. Underwood wasn't known as Deadly for nothing. From that angle off left arm round the wicket, the ball was flying over the batsmen's shoulders, a most unnerving sight when you are padded up and waiting for your medicine. That was the kind of thing that Underwood could do. Deliveries would explode off the surface and he would be absolutely unplayable.

And so we rejoin at the point where I asked Charlie for that advice.

'I'd just have a swipe, if I were you,' he said.

I walked in at 32 for six, Underwood ended up with figures of 10.1-7-9-6, Lancashire were 62 all out and Kent were already 180 runs ahead with four wickets left standing by the close of day one. Declaring early next day, they won by an innings, without the use of day three. Underwood finished with 10 wickets in the match. Just have a swipe, indeed.

It just goes to show how coaching has changed over the years. Overall, however, I had a strong relationship with Charlie. He clearly took to me because I was a left-hander like him, and we also used to have another thing in common, as former footballers with Rossendale United. A now-defunct football club whose ground was called Dark Lane. Or in modern parlance, The Stadium of Dark. I'm sure that's where Sunderland got the name from.

Coaches in this period would do their work when play stopped rather than during the course of a match. They would sit and talk to you, and try to improve your game that way. These blokes were more like mentors. They wouldn't do any technical coaching with you. They wouldn't be in the nets alongside you like a Duncan Fletcher, unpicking technique; just sit and talk and try to improve your game that way. Particularly when you got out. It was then that you would be asked to describe how you got out and to build the picture of how things looked from your vantage point. As the ball came down, how had you reacted to the picture that you were seeing? What might you do if you were faced with that kind of scenario again, so that a different result might be reached? Could you have played a different shot? They looked after you, tried to offer you their experience and they wanted you to succeed.

From a player's perspective, there will always be respect for elders who have played international cricket and Norman

'Buddy' Oldfield had featured for England, and would surely have won more caps but for the fact that his single one came in 1939 in what was the final Test before the Second World War. Scores of 80 and 19 versus West Indies would have provided a strong argument for retention in the XI but a six-year hiatus was followed by an inability to agree new terms with Lancashire. Not until 1948, with Northamptonshire, did Buddy resume his career. His subsequent return to Manchester came in 1968 and he would go on to replace Hallows as coach.

However, Buddy felt more like a mate than the other two. Perhaps this was how the position of coach was evolving. For example, one time after we had spent all day out in the field, Buddy, whose nervous demeanour included tendencies to blink uncontrollably as well as stutter, began a dressing-room debrief by telling the bowling attack they had not performed so well. Jim Cumbes, one of the seamers in his sights, picked up this slightest of men and hung him on one of the coat hooks, leaving his legs kicking underneath. It was a light-hearted moment. And it shows the difference between the team atmospheres now and those of 50 years ago. These coaches were treated like your pals whereas nowadays the relationship is more of a professional one.

By this time there were also assistant coaches coming on board, although the extent of the coaching from men like Ralph Alderson tended to be comparable to fatherly advice. Unlike the other three I've mentioned, Ralph was not an England player. In fact, he only played a couple of first-class matches and combined his role at Old Trafford with running a pub in Bolton. Invariably he would turn up late and in his distinctive Lancastrian drawl would say: 'I'm terribly sorry, coach. We just had a delivery and I had to wait until all the barrels had been packed away.'

Jack Bond, our captain at that time, was as good as anyone with his advice on batting. He would tell me: stand up, you're crouched. Taking a crouched position at the crease means your eyes are at an angle looking down the pitch whereas if you stand up your eyes point straight down the middle of it.

A good modern example of this was David Warner in the 2019 Ashes when he kept getting too far over to the off-side when Stuart Broad was coming around the wicket. His eyes were at an angle, which meant he wasn't ever aligning himself to play the ball properly and Broad was therefore getting the ball through him for fun. Although Warner kept fiddling about with his guard: leg stump, middle, off stump. It wasn't where he started that was the problem. It was where he was ending up – as he fell across one way, the ball was coming the other and was cleaning him up. He was never really in line with it.

It was one of Jack Bond's big things for a batsman to be standing up straight. Advice is always more valuable from someone that's been there and gone through the same struggles.

Players these days have got it on a plate. They can go and see how they have got out immediately after an innings is over, stop the video clip, slow it down, and even freeze it right at the moment of impact. 'Look at your front leg, it's dead stiff, it's got to be bent.' That kind of thing.

Coaching is not done in the nets as much as on an iPad, but there were movements to go this way as far back as the early 1990s from an England perspective, and the first person I saw do it was actually Geoffrey Boycott.

When Micky Stewart was the England coach taking the team to the West Indies in 1989–90, he invited Boycs to get the players into the nets, mainly at Headingley, and provide them with an examination against fast bowling. And I mean genuinely fast bowling.

He got some lads to come in and bowl off about 18 yards, which made it feel as though they were bowling like lightning. He had a cine camera to film the likes of Michael Atherton, who was heading out on his first tour, and Alec Stewart playing against this extreme pace and, at the end of a session, he would take the film and show it to each of the individuals concerned. In his own inimitable way, of course.

Geoff was a pundit by this time and Micky was keen to use his knowledge and expertise. Micky really admired Boycott, who would invite the players: 'Come and sit with me. Now then, let's see what you're doing.' This was one of the first times a team was looking at video analysis as part of a training regime, albeit on fairly primitive equipment in modern terms. The batsmen weren't doing much more than ducking and weaving out of the way, but they could get a good look at how they were moving when rushed by extreme pace and that might be good for some.

Talking of primitive methods brings me to Brian Statham, one of Lancashire's greatest ever performers. The son of a dentist, who hailed from Gorton in Manchester, he played for England almost as long as he did for Lancashire, making his international debut just nine months after his county one and retiring in 1968, three years after a wicketless 70th and final Test appearance.

He was one of the most prolific bowlers on the county scene during this period, profiting from the old fast bowler's maxim of 'You miss, I hit'. His unerring accuracy kept the batsman under pressure.

And he lived by the theory that bowlers bowled themselves fit. A man of simple pleasures, with a liking for beer and cigarettes, he was a product of his age. Lancashire and other leading county clubs like Surrey had begun turning their attention to all-round fitness through specialist coaches. Not one for excessive physical preparation, however, Brian used to say that he would get himself fit for a season with a fortnight of bowling in the nets.

He would start in April, bowling with a couple of sweaters on, and by the time you saw him down to his shirt sleeves you knew that both one of England's finest exponents of seam bowling and the weather had warmed up.

Although his standards were high, the reality was that the team was in decline as his career came towards its conclusion. Lancashire finished next to bottom in the Championship table in 1962 and any progress year on year was gradual. It was a curiosity, in fact, that in consecutive years, the final standings for the club were 16th, 15th, 14th, 13th, 12th and 11th.

New players were emerging, however, as Jack Bond took over the captaincy in 1968. Ones with more modern characteristics such as John Sullivan, who embodied the 'bits and pieces' tag familiarly given to cricketers ever since. He was able to contribute with bat or ball. He would never score a hundred or take a five-wicket haul in first-class cricket, but his cameos were often priceless. There were also two fast bowlers who would go on to play for England in Ken Shuttleworth and Peter Lever, who stepped up when Statham stepped down.

Yet it was two players invited to play a bit of second XI cricket in 1968 who would prove influential in the club's rise. Jack Simmons had missed out on a contract at the age of 21 and had since been on decent money as a draughts-man for Lancashire County Council. Aged 27, he jumped at the chance of a return, and when selected for the match versus Derbyshire in Derby was asked to pick someone up at Haslingden because he had a car. That someone was Clive Lloyd. A teammate of Jack's that week and for several hun-dred weeks thereafter. At that time a player from overseas had to do a qualifying period before playing county cricket and that meant serving time in the local leagues as well as the club's stiffs.

Their arrivals on the scene dovetailed with the advent of the John Player League. Both suited limited-overs cricket. Clive, who I affectionately refer to as my brother from another mother, played his shots and his attitude rubbed off. He promoted adventure. Jack, meanwhile, could bat a bit and his bowling was as tight as a snare drum. It was a powerful combination in 40-over matches.

Few players to have walked out with the red rose on their chest have been as popular as Jack. He reckoned he would have walked from Accrington to Manchester to sign his first contract at the end of the 1968 season, for the following year. 'I was earning more as a draughtsman, but I don't care. There was no need for negotiations when they told me they wanted to take me on. It was just "sign here, son",' he said of his £750 deal. His previous higher income had been supplemented by money for pro-ing in the Ribblesdale League at weekends. But playing for Lancashire had been a dream.

Jack made up for his late arrival by staying for the next 20 years, and didn't want to stop either, after convincing himself he could have gone on to his 50th birthday. He had been named as a *Wisden* Cricketer of the Year at the age of 44, for goodness sake, and took in excess of 60 first-class wickets in both 1987 and 1988. But Lancashire told him he had to finish to allow the next generation to come through.

He had first played for the first team as an amateur, which was very unusual by then, and took his chance when given opportunities. John Savage, the first-choice off-spinner, was left out to give Jack experience in the early-season contest versus Oxford University in 1969; the understudy claimed seven wickets and never relinquished his place in the team. He played his second competitive match at the age of 28 and went on to make 450 first-class appearances and a further 471 in List A cricket.

That is a huge number of lunches and teas. A wage cut might have been taken to go full time, but at least he wasn't having to fork out for his meals. None of which he ever wanted to sacrifice. Take our matches at out-grounds, for example. Keen to make an impression in what was a limited time frame, the locals would put on a decent spread but if things were running late, the players weren't the caterers' priority. The special guests would get the special treatment and us players would be finishing up after the umpires had dinged the bell for a resumption.

'I am not coming onto the field before I have had my gooseberry tart,' Jack insisted one day at Blackpool.

Jack certainly carried a bit of excess timber, but he was fit enough to maintain excellent standards for a full 21 years, and he regularly won his wagers with Ian Botham. The pair of them got on famously, both enjoying life to the full, and would weigh in when coming up against each other in Somerset v Lancashire fixtures. Whichever of the pair lost the most pounds between then and their next meeting in domestic cricket would have extra pounds in his wallet.

Goodness knows how Jack shed it because every April as a team we would go on a three-to-four-mile run through the streets surrounding Old Trafford. Not a great runner, as you can imagine, he always took something to take his mind off it. On one occasion he had a copy of the *Manchester Evening News* under his arm because he'd spotted a property that he wanted to buy and it was on the run route.

And he was regularly taking on extra fuel. Take away trips to the south coast. I would travel with Jack in the '70s, as we lived close by, and if we left at lunchtime there would be a takeaway stop immediately, followed by another around London – and there'd still be an evening meal on the cards that night.

Clayton Street Chippy, a fish-and-chip shop at Great

Harwood, has a signature dish that consists of a fish sat atop a steak pudding, chips, peas and gravy. A combo that came together all because of Jack's indecision. Unable to decide between meat and fish, he had both – with chips and mushy peas to accompany it, of course. It was known from then onwards as the 'Simmo Special'.

Lancashire had not won anything for a quarter of a century but the newly introduced short-format games suited our style. We became the Manchester United of cricket in this era, winning four Gillette Cup finals in 1970, 1971, 1972 and 1975. Inaugural John Player League champions in 1969, we also retained the silverware on the way to completing a double in 1970.

Jack Bond was the man who held everything together, having been plucked from the second XI at the age of 35 and made captain. He reckoned he was 'the only one daft enough'. But he was like that other Jack, Collier at Accrington, in his encouragement of young players like myself, Barry Wood and David Hughes. He wasn't just our captain. He was so much more: a mentor, a friend, who helped so many of us fulfil our potential and play international cricket. We all loved him and we all played for him. He was a great judge of mood; a fine reader of a situation. If you required an arm around the shoulder, it would be applied with minimum fuss. Step out of line and the bollocking would take place in the corner of the dressing room, away from others' prying eyes, and might be followed by a quiet beer. His shout, of course.

His leadership skills certainly rubbed off on me when he identified yours truly as his successor in 1973. And I know

Clive Lloyd took on board the way he conducted himself when considering what kind of captain of the West Indies he wanted to be. Jack described himself as an 'ordinary lad' rather than one of the lads. In truth, he was a father figure. A devout Christian who sang in the church choir, his outlook on life was similar to that of my own dad.

His guidance sometimes involved getting the team over the line, as in the twilight semi-final of 1971 at Old Trafford. David Hughes's incredible 24 runs from one over from John Mortimore, the Gloucestershire off-spinner, combined with light diminishing rapidly and the BBC holding back the *Nine O'Clock News*, left Jack with just a single to end the longest game in one-day history and book the Lord's final appearance, to the delight of over 20,000 fans.

At Lord's he took the spectacular, decisive catch off Jack Simmons's bowling that dismissed Kent's danger man Asif Iqbal to claim the Gillette Cup. Then, 12 months later, another instinctive Bond move was crucial in retaining the trophy. Clive Lloyd was asked to open the bowling with his right-arm filth in the final, a decision that allowed us to play an extra batsman. Warwickshire collected just 31 runs off his 12 overs, and Clive later struck a jaw-dropping 126.

Our other overseas player of that era, Farokh Engineer, was another who liked to play his shots. He certainly had more success locating the boundary than he did opposition grounds. He was famous for getting lost.

Legend has it that his hundred for India against Sir Garfield Sobers' West Indies in Madras in January 1967 was the fastest in Test history. Or at least Farokh says it was, coming from

46 balls. Records at that time only carried the minutes taken rather than deliveries faced and so it is not recognised in the history books. What is indisputable, however, is that against an attack of the quality of Wes Hall, Charlie Griffith, Sobers and Lance Gibbs, he surged to 94 not out by lunch. His opening partner, Dilip Sardesai, was dealing almost exclusively in singles for his 28, and Farokh had scored 109 of the 145 on the scoreboard when he was third out two hours 35 minutes into the match.

It was an innings that earned him acclaim, though, and a lucrative deal as Brylcreem's poster boy in India. Denis Compton and Keith Miller were the English and Australian equivalents.

You could not help but warm to Farokh and he is still revered in Manchester now – as is Clive Lloyd for that matter, each of them making the city their home. He had friends in high places, too. George Best became a good pal as they lived not far from each other. And news that he had become a father for the first time was delivered by none other than Her Majesty Queen Elizabeth.

Ahead of the Lord's Test of 1967, the Indian team was to be introduced to the Queen. That morning a telegram had been sent from Bombay to the Clarendon Court Hotel, opposite the ground, and it had been passed on to Billy Griffith, the then secretary of the MCC, who was stood on the outfield next to the Queen. He passed it to her in turn and she walked up to Farokh and said: 'Engineer, I have got some wonderful news for you.' He replied that he had been expecting it.

'What did you want, a boy or a girl?' she asked him.

'A girl.'

'Well, you've got one.'

These kinds of things happened to Farokh. Take the occasion of the 1983 World Cup final when he was in as summariser for the BBC's *Test Match Special* and, with India on the cusp of victory, Brian Johnston asked him whether the then Prime Minister of India, Indira Gandhi, would declare a public holiday if it was completed.

He had a good sense of humour did Farokh and, tongue-in-cheek, said that if she was listening he was sure she would grant one. Within minutes a message was received from Mrs Gandhi's office and relayed to the *TMS* team that she had heard their comments and had indeed declared a holiday. When they next met, she thanked him as she reckoned the gesture had earned her a few more votes.

My opening partner in that team was a Yorkshireman, who was superb against quick bowling, in Barry Wood. Perhaps it was because he was so fast on his feet? You see, he used to turn up for training sessions in hobnail boots, arguing that wearing them made his cricket boots feel so much lighter in matches.

I used to rib him on his all-round sporting prowess. He came over the Pennines with a reputation (entirely of his own fanfare) for being good at everything and then appeared to deconstruct the myths of being a fine runner, tennis player, footballer, whatever. But to be fair, Barry was a big-game player. Someone who influenced results of matches, as shown by his 15 man of the match awards in limited-overs contests prior to leaving the club for

Derbyshire in 1980. The following year, as captain, he led them to their maiden one-day trophy at Lord's with victory over Northamptonshire.

It was at this time that I swapped a Yorkie for a local lad as first-wicket partner. Graeme 'Foxy' Fowler was one of my great muckers at Old Trafford and a seriously good player. For me, to keep an eye out for him was to look after one of our own; I was absolutely thrilled to bits that this lad from Accrington had broken through into the Lancashire first team. He would later move to play his league cricket for Rawtenstall but had emerged from my town and my lifelong club.

Foxy was a bloke who could play any sport. Anything with a racquet. A batter who could adjust to all sorts of conditions and various types of bowlers; someone who took a hundred off the great West Indies attack of 1984 and a double hundred less than a year later off India in Madras in what proved to be the 20th and penultimate match of his international career. The mystery was that he finished that tour of India with a fifty and never played again. Less of a mystery, I suppose, when you consider that the rebel tourists of 1981–82, including Graham Gooch, became available again soon afterwards.

What made him different was his flexibility. He was like a rubber man. A brilliant fielder, he could keep wicket, and did so for England, but only as a stand-in and it wasn't his strong point. But he would play shots for people to marvel at. I would stand at the other end and think: 'How the hell has he done that?'

He was so rubbery with his hands and wrists that he could hit a left-arm spinner with a slog sweep high over midwicket. At that juncture in the late 1970s I had not seen that before. If I wanted to hit a left-arm spinner, I had to go down the pitch, get momentum as I did so and hit the ball over mid-on. Fowler could stand there and just go 'bang'. He was only a little bloke, but he would slam it square like you wouldn't believe.

It was far from a common shot at that time. History may even show that the slog sweep was yet to be invented but he was playing it, all right. Additionally, he was brave as you like against any pace bowler.

As opening partners, we never stopped talking in the middle. He was great company. Some people don't like conversing too much in the middle between overs, but I always liked a chat and our batting was effectively an extension of our off-field relationship. We travelled to games together, too, and would play the music turned up to levels you wouldn't believe. We got things rocking to such an extent that the bloody car used to shake.

Top of the play list was Bruce Springsteen & the E Street Band and Southside Johnny & the Asbury Jukes. Music was a big thing for him. A singer in the Lancashire youth choir, he also played drums – and like Phil Collins he used to like singing and drumming simultaneously. With mixed results I would say, if his performance at one Professional Cricketers' Association charity night was anything to go by. On that occasion he managed to mess up Steve Harley & Cockney Rebel's 'Come Up And See Me, Make Me Smile'. He only went and missed the huge pause in the middle, triggering a shedload of folk to scream at him: 'Have you never heard this flipping song?'

As mad as a box of frogs was Fowler. In fact, if it was his turn to get us to the ground (he only lived 200 yards away from me and as I lived in a cul-de-sac there was no obvious form of escape), he would just appear somewhere in our house. One morning, he burst in through the porch, ran up the steps to the front door, opened it and didn't break stride until he had burst into the bedroom and jumped in bed with my missus. Thankfully he had all his clothes on, but it still drew some Hammer Horroresque screams. Seconds later, natural as anything, he hopped in the car and off we drove to Old Trafford.

It's been so sad to see that such a life-and-soul kind of guy has had mental health issues in later life. He's talked a lot about them and it has been a good thing for him to open up by writing and lecturing about the subject, using his own experiences. Reaching out to people to show them how he has felt and how it has changed him – and I am not talking about the bloody big beard he's kept, which makes him look a bit like a slim David Bellamy.

The serious point about Foxy is that he was a confident bloke, someone always willing to speak his mind and not someone I would ever have envisaged suffering from depression. And how he has suffered. It is good to bump into him around cricket grounds because of what we've been through in our past. His life changed at the age of 47. Don't get me wrong, he copes, but like a lot of people with this affliction he has good days and bad days.

A dressing room needs all kinds of characters to be a successful one and during his playing days Foxy certainly was one of a kind. When he left the field he didn't take any of his troubles, should he have any, with him. Kit off, switch off used to be the way he was and that kind of attitude can be helpful to others. If everyone is sat around uptight about their latest failures – and let's face it cricket comes with a higher percentage of low scores and moderate bowling successes than hundreds and five-fors – it would be a fairly morbid habitat.

As a player he had exactly the right balance for high-end competition. He had great skill as a batsman that made opponents fearful and also a wit and humour that made him popular with his own team. He was also a hit with the fairer sex. In his youth, he was such a good-looking lad. Women would always be double-taking when we were out and about and they were never looking at me. The one time I recall the breaking of this rule it turned out the admirer in question had a bit of a lazy eye. So it goes.

It never showed with him, remaining rake-thin and as fit as a fiddle, but Foxy seemed to have a liking for wedding cake. He just kept getting married.

Our own union remained strong as Lancashire's opening pair. 'Alone we can do so little, together we can do so much' the saying goes and never was this more applicable than in the extraordinary match at the start of the summer holidays in 1982 when Lancashire hosted Warwickshire at Southport.

Merseyside melted under a sapping sun and, after the ignominy of following a full day chasing the ball all over the field at Trafalgar Road, I was dismissed at its fag end by Gladstone Small.

To put things into context here, Alvin Kallicharan and Geoff Humpage had struck double hundreds during a stand of 470, a record for the fourth wicket in Championship cricket as the visitors eventually declared on 523. It left them enough time to dismiss me before the close of play on what was the friendliest of batting surfaces. To apply the proverbial salt, I was left to reflect on the fact that anyone can fall to the new ball not from the pavilion but the non-striker's end as Fowler's runner.

As a team, we took advantage of Small missing a large chunk of the next day – in a quirk of this rather odd match, the Warwickshire manager David Brown filled in as substitute, was allowed to bowl under the circumstances and took a wicket – as an emergency standby for Derek Pringle on international duty. While Small was making what proved to be a wasted round trip to Edgbaston, Lancashire were piling up a decent score in his absence, with muggins here playing a rather unwanted part.

Foxy hit 126, a round 100 of them on the second day, despite being hampered by a thigh muscle injury, allowing my namesake Clive Lloyd to declare 109 runs behind. A decision that invited Warwickshire to show how the third innings of a match can be a team's Achilles heel.

Les McFarlane, a West Indian bowler recruited following his release from Northamptonshire a couple of years earlier, had the match of his life, taking six wickets, despite there being very little on offer in the surface and, despite the pummelling we had taken at the start of the contest, it left a victory target of 221.

'I am not getting out again, someone else will have to run for you this time,' I told Fowler before we set off on our pursuit.

Rather than watching, I fancied playing a more active role in proceedings this time and if I was going to be doing any running it would be for my own personal cause. An unbeaten 88, coupled with Foxy's second hundred of the game, saw us to the most unlikely of 10-wicket wins. It was one of two first-class matches in my career in which I was to barely leave the field. The other? The Test match against India in Birmingham, and my career zenith, when I struck an unbeaten 214.

During the first of his winters away with England, on the Ashes tour of 1982–83, Foxy was selected to room with Chris Tavare for the first few weeks. Some time had been allowed for the team to bond and so partners, like Tavare's wife Vanessa, were not permitted.

When asked how they had got on in their quarters, it was discovered that they had proved to be ships in the night.

'When I get in, he's asleep. And when I wake up he's dressed and gone. All I see is this pair of pyjamas neatly folded on the pillow,' Fowler said.

That was Foxy, one of the most social creatures that I came across on the county circuit.

He had a wicked wit, too. For example, later on that same tour, some medical students from Queensland pulled a prank in which they smuggled a piglet into a one-day international at the Gabba and released it onto the field during Australia's innings.

Daubed on one side of the porker was EDDIE, a reference to England off-spinner Hemmings, and on the other BOTHAM, the banter being that this pair represented the tourists' fat club.

It meant they became the butt of Australian jokes. Neither were they safe from internal piss-taking as Fowler proved when on one occasion, as the team strolled to its transport for the day, Hemmings was outed for his dawdling. 'For Christ's sake, Eddie, put your trotter down,' he was told.

There was a serious side to his dedication to cricket, though, revealed in the outstanding work he carried out in his post-playing career. The number of young cricketers he helped mentor and progress into first-class and international players during his development of Durham University's Centre of Excellence was incredible. He produced a real conveyor belt of talented cricketers. Those of the ilk of James Foster, Nick Compton and not least Andrew Strauss. No wonder five other universities in Oxford, Cambridge, Loughborough, Leeds and Cardiff replicated the model he put in place over 19 years up in the North-east.

They clearly recognised good coaching and a nurturing approach to it. We all have slightly different ideas on how to be the best coach you can when you are trying to mould emerging players into finished products, but the one thing I liked in the Fowler approach was the desire to be 'the coach that I would have wanted to have as a player'.

Foxy has experienced lots of facets of the game and every

single layer of its structure from grassroots to the very top. He came through the system in the 1970s and '80s and then helped in the development of undergraduates to county professionals across two decades. He also has his experience of maintaining wellness off the field.

During his latter playing days he was a Durham teammate of Ian Botham, and they live not so far apart as well. The pair were always close and it has been a kind-hearted and merited move by Beefy, who is chairman of Durham somehow, to take him on as a mentor to the club's players and coaches. That was a grand gesture and also one from which others will benefit.

Fowler came through the Lancashire system with his Durham University mate Paul Allott. They were like two musketeers in their youth. Allott was in reality one of those medium-fast bowlers who would keep you honest. But in his head he was Frank Tyson and had a temper to match.

On one occasion, Fowler was at slip and floored one. Now, nobody ever means to drop a catch, and if you are stood at slip it is generally because you are the best, or at least one of the best, fielders in the side. But Allott went marching down the pitch like only Allott could, with his splayed feet making their distinctive prints at ten-to and ten-past the hour, and demanded: 'Get that f***ing bloke out of there. I'm not bowling another ball until he f***ing moves!'

It sounds totally against any kind of team ethos one might recognise in modern terms, but it's the kind of thing you could do to a mate in our day.

Most recently, Walt – as he is known in the game by virtue

of one of his middle names being Walter – has moved on to the Lancashire County Cricket Club Board and his new stimulation in life is to return silverware to Old Trafford as director of cricket. It didn't surprise me when he took up this position in 2018 as he is one of life's great organisers. If you want anything sorted, ask him. Yes, he will rub people up the wrong way but look past his abrasive nature and he gets things done. Things weren't any different when he was on the field. But he is a mate, and you can put up with all that for results.

Prior to this Allott was instrumental in the appointment of Glen Chapple as Lancashire's head coach. One of the best who has not had any kind of career for England was Glen. He played one one-day game versus Ireland but I saw how much talent he had first-hand because I was involved with Lancashire at that time.

Longevity was the key. He knew himself he needed to get fitter in order to perform and did so. He got stronger year on year and this was a man who knew how to enjoy himself. But he knew there was the time for enjoying yourself and the time for doing the business. He's been a massive asset to Lancashire, a club man through and through.

The one thing about his style of bowling was that if there was anything in the pitch, because of his accuracy he would find it and everybody in the country knew that. In domestic finals at Lord's – matches we made a habit of appearing in during the 1990s – he was a real handful because he would hit the spot and allow the ball to do its thing.

Lancashire have had a tradition of the Chapple-type of

bowler – Ken Higgs, Allott, Jimmy Anderson and most recently Tom Bailey. Hit-the-deck bowlers, quick enough to keep a batsman honest and reliant on accuracy. I still see Glen on a regular basis; he's in his forties but looking as if he could still play. One thing I know is that if Darren Stevens can still play, so could Chapple, and he would do the business.

To be honest, I am not sure what my old mate David Green would make of Stevens' running style. But I know that he wouldn't have made him an exception to his commentaries. No one was safe in our house of fun. And that ensured that I look back on what was a turbulent time behind the scenes at Old Trafford – with the loss of Peter Marner and Geoff Clayton from the playing staff, the removal of an entire committee and the departure of the club secretary Geoffrey Howard to Surrey – fondly.

As a young player, problems tended to go over my head, but I reckon I was a quick learner. To survive in a professional club with a playing staff of 28, you needed to develop some personality as well as sound batting and bowling techniques. And it was an environment that suited me.

The pressure of having to live up to the highest of standards was not there as the club had not won trophies since the 1950s. That kind of pressure was elsewhere. Just over the Pennines, in fact, with a club that I developed a fascination with from an adolescent age.

CHAPTER 5

The White Rose

Brian Close was the heartbeat of the Yorkshire team that won seven titles in 10 years from 1959 onwards. No other team in history has dominated the County Championship like they did during this era.

Even before his official appointment as captain in 1963, he was directing traffic out on the field, his sharp cricket brain and impulsive, intuitive decisions integral to how this machine of a side operated.

As an opponent you could feel their parts working in unison to grind you down, which was quite something, not least because Yorkshire County Cricket Club and friction have proved as compatible as gin and tonic over the years. As a Lancastrian cricketer, it was tough to have to admit that the old enemy from over the hill was better than us.

Yet at that time in English cricket's cycle they just were. They were better than everybody when they wanted to be, and well led.

Yes, Close was good tactically although some may suggest his ideas bordered on bonkers. He was a lead-from-the-front sort of player whether he was wearing the captain's armband or not, and was actually known to alter field settings from the ranks. It was said that Ronnie Burnet was okay with this but his successor Vic Wilson, who took over in 1960, not so.

If his leadership – which took effect after one Championship pennant was claimed under Burnet and two under Wilson – was inspirational, it also proved unconventional at times. He was always tinkering and moving the field, trying to put opponents off. Sometimes he would stand under batsmen's noses just to get them thinking about what he was doing, and not about the ball that was coming down to them any second.

If they kept their concentration and thwacked him on his person with attacking strokes, no matter. In fact, while the kind of blows he took may have forced other men off the field, he wore them as badges of honour. 'Pain, it's only in the mind,' he used to say.

In 1976, when he was brought back by England to face the full might of the West Indies at Old Trafford, I was one of those watching – stood under the bell in the members' end, with a pint in hand. I'd played for England the year before but was now out of the picture.

Tony Greig had taken over the captaincy from Mike Denness and brought David Steele and Close in. The West Indies pace trio of Andy Roberts, Michael Holding and Wayne Daniel were bowling like the wind at Closey. So fast that stood side-on in front of the Old Trafford pavilion, you couldn't see the trajectory of the ball. And, undeterred,

Closey's going forward and taking it on his chest. To be fair, English bats hardly made contact at all. Extras, the only other contributor in double figures behind Steele's 20 in the first innings, top-scored with 25 in the second.

That match proved to be the 22nd and final one of a Test career for Close that began in 1949 and spanned 11 different series. His unorthodoxy at times frustrated people. For example, take the Ashes Test at Old Trafford in 1961 when he decided to take on the Australian leg-spinner Richie Benaud and try to hit him out of the attack. When that gamble backfired, he drew quite a lot of criticism. Jim Laker was to call it 'the most extraordinary innings I've ever seen by an accredited Test batsman'.

The archetypal Yorkshireman, he was a stubborn bugger. But a brave one, too. As I mentioned, he loved getting whacked and Tony Greig used to delight in telling the story of playing alongside him in that era. An era of uncovered pitches. If Derek Underwood came on, bowling on a wet 'un, Close would be at short leg, and Greig would be at silly point.

They would both be damn near stood on the pitch – not actually on it as you can't stand there, you're not allowed to – but they were right up as far as they could legally get. With his long arms, Greig's hands would often be underneath the batsman and on the other side of the pitch was Close, the human blockade.

They say good cricketers always think outside the box for the little advantages that might lead to a batsman being dismissed. An unusual field placing, a different line of attack from the bowler. Close, meanwhile, devised one of the craziest plans ever attempted on a cricket field.

'When they sweep,' he would say, referring to the batsmen, 'if I don't duck, it could hit me on the head. Keep alert and watch the ball because you could get the ricochet. There is every chance it will rebound across the pitch.'

At Yorkshire, he would set his teammates ridiculously tall tasks, such as telling openers Phil Sharpe and Ken Taylor to give it a thrash. On one occasion he apparently demanded: 'I want a hundred runs in the next forty minutes. Don't get out and don't make it look easy!' Right you are, then.

Those instructions, while ludicrous in the extreme, nevertheless revealed something of Close's mindset. He had a well-known theory during his time in charge. Winning County Championship matches was not primarily down to how many runs you made, how long you could spend compiling intimidating totals. Often competitive ones would suffice because what was most relevant in a three-day match was the time you required to bowl the other team out for a second time. Close was one of those captains who believed it was better to lose occasionally – while trying to win – than settle for dull stalemates and so was always trying to work towards a position of strength for that final day or final innings.

It was a decent formula judging by the results. Yorkshire won four Championships in six seasons of Close's captaincy, following the three in four they had won under Burnet and Wilson. He would have you believe all seven had been on his watch and, such was his personality, to some extent they had been.

Close, professional autograph hunter on that centenary trip to Australia, was an absolute one-off. Being from Lancashire, it's strange to admit that a lot of my favourite cricketers are Yorkshiremen, but it is true. There was so much to admire about this formidable team I first came up against in the mid-1960s, which included Ken Taylor, Geoff Boycott, Dougie Padgett, Phil Sharpe, Raymond Illingworth, Jimmy Binks, Fred Trueman, Tony Nicholson and Don Wilson. They were fantastic but they used to flipping argue like cat and dog all of them.

Close was captain, of course, but in the chairman Brian Sellers they had a man who could keep them all in check. One thing he would have had from them is respect as one of the club's most successful captains of the past. Six times in 10 seasons under his leadership, either side of the Second World War, Yorkshire were crowned county champions.

Sellers was a dour, proud, brilliant Yorkshireman, a proper 'now then' kind of bloke. When he walked into a room, he had a real presence, the kind that would make even Fred shut up. Not much else did, mind.

I was 18 when I first played against them in a Roses match at Bramall Lane, Sheffield. It was a week of wet weather, there was an uncovered pitch awaiting us and it got a bit tacky. Geoff Pullar, an England opening batsman and a bloody good player, was my mentor. I was due to go in at number seven and, before the first innings, Geoff said to me: 'Just forget Fred. He'll have plenty to say, sure, but he will have plenty to say before we've even started.'

This was a reference to the habit Fred made of coming into

our changing room pre-match with his pipe hanging out of the corner of his mouth, and going round everybody, lining his victims up for a spot of mental disintegration.

He would ask: 'Are you playing? That's one.'

Then, embarking on a tour of the pegs, would add: 'Are you? Two. You? Three. Four.'

Then came the big moment, as he settled his eyes upon me.

'Who's this young lad, then?'

'This is David Lloyd.'

'Can ye hook?

'Well ... I ...'

But before I had chance to mumble any more words, he was straight in with: 'Don't worry, you'll get plenty of opportunity today, lad.'

As a youngster making your way in the game, appearing in just your fourth first-class match, you're absolutely shitting bricks. But Geoff urged me to ignore the words as they weren't the things that could hurt me.

'Just keep playing forward on that pitch, it's a tacky one, there's no bounce in it, so he's not getting it up there, just keep playing forward.'

I kept that firmly in mind as Fred was steaming in and zipping the ball beyond my pushes onto the front foot, alternating between inside and outside edges. It just kept sinking into the gloves of wicketkeeper Jimmy Binks behind the stumps, causing Fred to put on the great theatre he was renowned for at the end of his run-up. Pulling up his pants in exasperation, rolling his sleeves up.

One intimidating character lurking 50 yards away and

another in the figure of Close standing, almost in my pocket, at short leg. You could sort of hear him breathing as the bat tapped at the earth beneath my feet. And he would not have been bothered in the slightest if I had clipped one straight into him, of course.

Turning to his strike bowler, he instructed him to bowl straight and Fred came back with 'How can I bowl straight, when I am swinging it this road and that? Late.'

What an experience a Roses match like this was. I didn't get any runs, bagging a pair. Twice caught by that man Close, off the left-arm spinner Don Wilson. But it offered a really good early grounding in my career. The rivalry, a ground packed to the rafters, lots of trepidation, mixing with legends of the game.

Closey was indestructible. Or he certainly acted as if he was. Years after that inauspicious first meeting in Sheffield, I was sat in his company at a formal dinner in Leeds. Wives accompanied the players on this occasion and so I'm sat opposite Mrs Close, Vivien, who played a part in shaping her husband's cricket ability. You see, Brian always maintained players should learn to ballroom dance because it kept them on their toes; he and Vivien danced together regularly. The problem was both of them wanted to lead, which doesn't work in ballroom dancing. There can only be one leader. Needless to say who won on that score.

Close always seemed to do things a bit unconventionally, and I was in hysterics when he revealed what he had been up to that week. We were talking away when he just declared: 'I got pulled up by the police, you know. Got nothing better to do, I suppose.'

At which point, he carried on troughing.

'Carry on with the story, Brian,' Vivien said.

'I am on the motorway, so I know it's seventy mile an hour, and I was doing eighty tops,' he continued.

'You can maybe tell everyone where you were and what you were towing.'

Turns out he was on the slip road of said motorway and pulling the caravan!

Close had issues with authority. And they him. Take the English hierarchy of the 1970s. The MCC still ran the national side and their colours were worn on overseas tours. He wasn't an MCC type of bloke, and despite an outstanding record of six wins and a draw from seven matches, his England captaincy was to prove brief due to the fact that he refused to apologise for a time-wasting episode in a county match.

That was unusual because it was normally his teams setting the pace. He would do anything to get ahead in a game. To advance a position. The burning question always: 'How do we win?'

That's where the unorthodoxy kicked in. He was always an advocate of having a swipe, a bit of a slog in a quest to get into a position from where the victory bid could be launched. But you also had to get him out more often than not. And he was a brave bastard, at his best in adversity, and when conditions were tough. When it was like that his attitude was, 'Yeah, I will roll my sleeves up and sort this out.'

He proudly showed the battle scars he received against the Windies fast bowlers of 1976 to the newspapers. Remember his autobiography was called *I Don't Bruise Easily.*

But he was fallible, as proved when Brian Sellers sacked him as Yorkshire captain in 1970 to promote Geoffrey Boycott. It is said that Sellers was to regret his action. 'It is the worst decision I've ever made in my life,' he is alleged to have told Close, who spent the final seven years of his playing career revitalising Somerset.

They absolutely loved him down at Taunton, where he had a massive influence on the young Ian Botham. Not least on journeys to and from matches, as they used to travel together in the car.

Closey always had a flask whenever they took a lengthy trip, and he would say to his young charge: 'Now then, Ian, lad, you can drive for a bit.'

It came as a bit of a shock, even to a daredevil sportsman like Botham when, on the first occasion such instructions were given, Close let go of the steering wheel and lunged for the flask. Botham's expectation had been that the car would be pulled over first.

'No, no,' Close said. 'You'll be fine while I just have a brew, it's all yours.'

No wonder Beef is barmy – he spent that much time with Closey when he was young. They also shared one common characteristic. Neither was ever wrong. Offering an alternative view was pointless. They were similarly gifted when it came to sport. As the country's youngest-ever Test cricketer, Close first played for England at 18; Botham at 20. Both played professional football.

Close could literally do anything. Bat, bowl, field. He could play golf right-handed and left-handed. Both to single figures. An all-action kind of guy immersed in this competitive world. He was Billy Whizz. Downtime would feature a study of the racing form. You rarely saw him away from the field of play without a copy of the *Sporting Life* under his arm.

My take is that Beefy saw this charismatic figure turn up claiming 'I can do anything' and wanted to be that man. I reckon he got all his chutzpah from Close. He made an even more significant intervention, too – he introduced Beefy to his wife Kath.

A bloke's bloke, one of his quirks was that he called everybody 'lad'. There would be Ian, lad. Arrive at the ground in Taunton and he would greet you: 'All right, David, lad?' And he didn't discriminate between the sexes, even calling Ethel, Somerset's tea lady, lad.

The stories of his bar-room party pieces while spending winters playing club cricket in South Africa are legendary. You may have seen an old-school trick in which competitors stand behind a line and are challenged to place beer bottles on the floor as far beyond the line as possible without either foot crossing it. The winner is the one placing an upright bottle the furthest.

Close, a towering man himself, would go up against these bloody big Afrikaners and crash through these skittles of glass in his bid to win. The same level of commitment was shown in the trick of holding a lit cigarette between your fingers. He would stick that longer than anybody else, no doubt reminding himself once again: 'Pain, it's only in the mind.'

All one need do to engage him was say: 'I bet you can't do this.'

And he finally met his match when a jet-heeled young kid challenged him with an extraordinary task. The footballer Duncan McKenzie famously used to jump over Minis and this was a variation on it as the lad took a run at the bar they were in and jumped over it, landing in the well where the bar staff served, stopping dead in the process.

Bold as brass, Close declared: 'Yep, I can do that.' So, he took a run at this bar, went straight through and crashed into the optics. There's bottles of whisky, there's gin, rum, all sent flying and he was laid out on the floor, awash with spirits. If nothing else, the whole crazy episode showed what a great competitor he was.

It never left him, either, as I found out at one Scarborough festival right at the end of my own career. Lancashire used to be regular participants in the end-of-season Fenner Trophy. There were other fixtures scheduled during that week, too, and it was always a fun time of the year for players to be involved. It was a bit of a jolly, truth be told, and night times were hectic.

This was the case when I was selected for the D. B. Close XI to play the touring Pakistanis in a one-day match in September 1982. I was stationed at mid-on and Desmond Haynes was at mid-off, wearing one of those wide-brimmed hats Australians are so fond of dangling corks from.

We were still suffering the effects of a particularly long night, and Norman Gifford, the left-arm spinner, was bowling when Mohsin Khan had an almighty dip at a particular delivery and the ball towered skyward and dropped between us. Neither of us reacted particularly well to it being hit there;

we were looking at each other in the way two drivers might after a bump at a roundabout.

Out of the corner of my eye, I noticed a figure striding towards us. It was Close, our captain, who gave myself and Desmond just about the biggest bollocking we've ever had.

'This is a f***ing Test match,' he bellows.

No, it wasn't. But we understood the point he was trying to get at. We had been chosen in a representative XI against a touring team.

'I cannot have you messing about like that. If you carry on like this, I will send you off! You have let this bloke off the hook,' he continued.

What can you say in that situation, apart from: 'Sorry, skip.'

Closey was 51 and he was still taking it mega seriously. Then again, it was only five years on from his most recent England recall.

One of the men who played under Close at Yorkshire was to become a brilliant captain in his own right. In late 1968, Ray Illingworth had asked for the security of a three-year contract at Headingley and was given short shrift by Sellers. Standard contracts tended to be 12 months in length but the establishment of the Professional Cricketers' Association that year provided individuals with greater confidence about their worth. Illingworth knew his, and accepted Leicestershire's offer to become their club captain.

Within four weeks of the following season, when Colin Cowdrey tore an Achilles, Illy was captain of England. Within a further 18 months, he was an Ashes-winning captain on Australian soil. In 1975, Leicestershire won their maiden Championship title.

I had the greatest respect for everything Illy achieved as a player and as a captain, and the credentials listed above were good enough to justify him becoming England supremo – as the position of manager and chairman of selectors effectively made him – in the 1990s.

He had a wonderful cricket brain and possessed a better sense of humour than people gave him credit for, so was not as curmudgeonly as some would have him portrayed. One of his failings, however, was that his way was always right. As a captain this worked. He moulded his teams as he saw fit.

But when he became coach and manager he wanted to maintain that status quo and that, at times, made things difficult, not least because he had a captain to contend with, and a strong minded-one at that, in Michael Atherton. Illingworth the player would not have stood for that and there was friction between them. The bottom line was they were very similar. Both passionate, with strong ideas, something had to give. It rarely did.

What I must say, though, is that Raymond was only ever absolutely fair with me from the moment I was asked in the spring of 1996, during Lancashire's pre-season tour of the Caribbean, to become England coach.

As a player, I found him an engaging opponent and a wonderful captain, someone always engrossed in the game from a tactical point of view. His style of captaincy would have evolved from the bits he picked up from Close, Ronnie Burnet, who was a real leader of men, and Sellers, whose iron fist I am sure would have rubbed off in some way.

He was certainly very astute in the recruitment of players he wanted to sign for the club. They tended to be experienced guys from around the country. With the help of a visionary secretary in Mike Turner, who had persuaded Illingworth himself to move to Grace Road and had previously recruited the ex-Surrey spinner Tony Lock, he attracted the likes of Chris Balderstone and Jack Birkenshaw from Yorkshire, John Steele from Staffordshire, Barry Dudleston from Cheshire and Ken Higgs, who was then a pro in the Lancashire League. They won the title in 1975 without a single homegrown player in their regular XI.

Tactically, Illy left no stone unturned. Take his pre-match inspections as an example. Most people would consider tactics to be a reactive response to the happenings on the field during the course of a game. Not him. He would be pre-empting things even before a ball was bowled, and it would be normal practice to turn up at an away ground, assess the pitch and the playing area and – if he was unhappy with any element of what he saw – demand change.

'That boundary is not long enough,' he might challenge, if he was unhappy that the ropes had been brought in too far. Leicestershire often operated with three spinners in their team and it therefore suited them to play on grounds with big expanses of outfield, which is how their home base of Grace Road was. So he would make it his business to go to the umpires and demand that the boundary be taken back if possible.

Forget the fact that he wasn't on his home turf, he would

still argue the toss, and more often than not with justification. He would carry around the written directives from the Test and County Cricket Board and, finger rubbing up against the regulation in question, would wave said book under the noses of the officials.

'There you are,' he would insist, should Leicestershire arrive at any venue where the home team had wilfully reduced the dimensions.

'They can go back another fifteen or twenty yards.' And he would make sure that the adjustments he proposed happened.

That revealed something of his thick skin. He didn't care what outsiders thought of him. As a Yorkshireman might say: 'Sod 'em.'

Not much credit was given to his softer side, though, or the care he showed for his teams. Taken by the warmth he felt towards him at Leicestershire, he had told the entire staff ahead of his first season in charge: 'Any grievances, don't let them out of this room. I want to look after you all.'

Players felt the strength of his loyalty and leadership on the field, too, most notably in what was the seventh Ashes Test of 1970–71 when John Snow's hostile bowling spell in Sydney deteriorated into a near riot and threatened a first forfeiture in Test cricket.

Snow, the primary weapon of Illingworth's bowling artillery, bowled an ideal length for Australian conditions – hitting the pitch hard, he would make it rise between chest and shoulder height. A really uncomfortable area to force a batsman to play but not one that should be interpreted as a bouncer.

What constituted such a delivery was a moot point throughout a series that England led 1-0 heading into this match with
Snow and the umpire Lou Rowan best described as being at
odds over it. The collective noun for lemurs is a conspiracy.
The term applied to a group of bouncers is intimidatory bowling, and intimidatory bowling would result in a warning to
the bowler and any repeat offence in removal from the attack.
The flashpoint arrived when Terry Jenner, Australia's number
nine, ducked into the line of a ball from Snow that struck
him on the head. After Jenner, a leg-spinner who would later
mentor Shane Warne, was helped from the field covered in
blood, Rowan considered it to be intimidatory and issued a
warning. Snow considered it to be multiple lemurs.

Of course, Illingworth was right in there to defend his
bowler as a row ensued and provide Rowan, the most officious of Australian officials, with a few penn'orth of his own
for good measure. But things really kicked off after Snow
completed the over and made his way down to the picket
fence at fine leg. Amid boos and jeers, one spectator negotiated the boundary and put his hands on the Englishman.
Beer cans and other objects were hurled onto the field of
play, some full, some empty, and as the missiles flew past his
players, Illingworth acted.

No team of his would be subjected to this kind of treatment. He directed them off the field and to the dressing
room for a full seven minutes before Rowan came to ask of
England's intentions. The question rather bluntly was: 'Is
your team coming back onto the field? Or are you forfeiting
the match?' Of course, they were going to return, and they

would go on to seal victory that would complete a 2-0 series win, one of only three by an England team on Australian soil in the past 50 years. Far from a climbdown by Illingworth, the strength of his resolve, and fact that he had effectively made the officials come to him to request a resumption, would have made a lasting impression on his teammates.

He clearly liked his players to play with a certain amount of aggression and didn't mind when personal rivalries, developed years previously, resurfaced in the interests of improving performance. When Leicestershire were in their ripest form, he took them into a contest against his native Yorkshire in Bradford and it meant Ken Higgs, who'd served Lancashire with such distinction, renewing acquaintances with Geoffrey Boycott.

Boycott was pushing forward and Higgs was probing away, zigzagging the ball past his outside edge repeatedly. The frustration was tangible for the bowler who started turning the air blue while telling his adversary exactly what he thought of his performance.

Not one to stand on ceremony, Boycs returned fire, causing the umpire Don Oslear to intervene. He spoke to Higgs. Alternately, he then had a few words with the batsman, a deliberate process designed to cool such a situation down. Or so he thought.

More heated expressions were exchanged and, after another couple of deliveries, Oslear wandered over to remind the visiting captain of the standards required in terms of behaviour on a cricket field. The message was clear. Get your man to stop gobbing off or there will be consequences.

Illingworth appeared to agree to the demands, and things seemed to be carrying on as normal, until he casually walked to the other umpire, Cec Pepper, at the end of the over and politely requested: 'Do me a favour: ask your mate over there not to interfere in private Roses battles.'

Illingworth's teams played tough cricket, all right. Indeed, John Steele once said to him: 'One of the things I enjoy most is taking to the field in the knowledge that other teams are frightened of us.' Leicestershire won the double of Championship and Benson & Hedges Cup in 1975, 12 months after claiming the Sunday League title.

And during their *annus mirabilis*, I was to fall victim to Illingworth's mickey-taking. At that time, there was a limit on the number of overs in the first innings of a Championship match. A forced declaration would occur at 100 overs and for the particular match in question – Lancashire v Leicestershire at Blackpool – that meant I was batting against the clock.

I scored a painstaking hundred, only managing to reach the mark in the 100th and final permitted over. I was captain of Lancashire and Ray was my opposite number and so it came to us to shake hands on a tame draw at the end of three days and three declarations. As we did so, he said to me: 'I've got to tell you, that's the worst hundred I've ever seen!'

How nice of him to say so. To be honest, I had to agree with him. It was a scratchy do to say the least. But the runs were on the board, and I added 90 more in the second innings before being dismissed.

As an off-spinner Illy's record was outstanding. In 787 first-class matches – one more than Close, the best man at his wedding – he took 2,072 wickets at a cost of 20.27 runs each. Quite simply, bowlers like him on uncovered pitches were dynamite.

What made Ray more dangerous than your average off-spinner, however, was the fact that he had a beautiful drifter – a delivery that provided his bowling with a nice variation and a significant threat.

Whereas with his orthodox off-spin his hand would come over the top of the ball and his fingers impart the revolutions on it, when he wanted it just to go on and not turn into the right-hander he would flatten his wrist. When he did so, the ball would just drift towards slip. The change in action was not straightforward to pick up either, which made it incredibly difficult to detect and even more effective.

Of his off-spinning rivals, the long-serving Middlesex bowler Fred Titmus also possessed a beautiful drifter while the other two of this era to use such a similar delivery successfully were Brian Langford of Somerset and Lancashire's own Jack Simmons.

It was a useful weapon to have. Illy would look to set you up as a batsman with a combination of off-spinner, off-spinner, off-spinner, drifter. It was not dissimilar in its appearance, execution and effectiveness to the 1990s phenomenon of the doosra, the delivery made popular by spinners such as Saqlain Mushtaq and Muttiah Muralitharan. For most people, not blessed with double-jointed parts to their bodies, producing one while maintaining a legitimate action was nigh-on impossible.

While Close and Illingworth were renowned for their

contribution to team success – Yorkshire did not claim any silverware between the Gillette Cup triumph in 1969 under the former and the 1983 Sunday League success when the latter came out of retirement to marshal things at the age of 51 – another of their greats will always be remembered for his unerring pursuit of individual brilliance.

Yorkshire were potless in the eight years of Geoffrey Boycott's captaincy of the club. His own standards did not drop during this period – he finished top of the national batting averages in the first seven – yet this devotion to excellence was not reflected in collective results.

A couple of incidents in recent years are reflections of his dedication to batting, which is effectively a personal pursuit housed within a team environment. The goal of all batsmen worth their salt is to score hundreds, which has been the Boycott mantra. And it stands to reason that if one of your players scores a hundred, the likelihood is that the team makes a competitive score. The greater the number of competitive scores, the greater the chances of winning matches. Although this doesn't always follow, of course.

The first came at Geoffrey's second home, a house that backs onto a golf course in Paarl, South Africa, about one hour's drive north-east of Cape Town. He invited Michael Vaughan over for a round during England's Test tour and when Michael arrived he discovered two people sitting in the hallway. Turns out they had won one of the big auction prizes at a Yorkshire Cricket Club dinner, this particular prize being to spend a week at the Boycotts' place.

Boycs, meanwhile, is wandering around in a T-shirt. A

T-shirt of himself. On the front of it was a picture of the moment when he scored his 100th first-class hundred at Headingley, the first man in history to reach such a landmark in a Test match, against Australia in 1977. The sense of achievement and occasion for Boycott was enhanced by the fact he had done it on his home ground.

On the front of this shirt, top and bottom of the picture, it says: 'Were you there, when I got my 100th hundred?'

On the back it says: 'If you weren't, you should have been!'

That's Geoffrey all over. He spent his entire career trying to compile three-figure scores. It was his life work and he's talked about the process of making them and their importance ever since. Grinding them out was what he was all about. You could not question his application nor his productivity. In the history of the first-class game, only Jack Hobbs, Patsy Hendren, Wally Hammond and Phil Mead have raised their bats to celebrate the particular innings milestone more often.

And another example that I was involved with shows Boycott's pride at his achievements.

A Sky Sports viewer had corresponded and very kindly sent me two wonderful photographs of Yorkshire's finest fast bowler that ever drew breath, Fred Trueman, in full flow, side-on at the crease. Both A4 size, each signed by Fred himself. It was a wonderful gesture.

I happened to receive them while covering an international match at Lord's for Sky Sports and was subsequently showing them off to a few mates in the media centre. This was taking place at the back of the BBC *Test Match Special* box, which is just down from the Sky commentary box and studio, on the top tier. Sky and the Beeb never tend to be too far apart from each other at any of the UK's leading grounds.

Anyhow, Geoffrey is passing down the corridor that runs behind the boxes and to the stairs to access the floor below when he notices my new treasured possessions.

'How many of those have you got?' he asks me.

'I've got two as it happens.'

He continued: 'Well. You don't need two, do you?!'

'Would you like one, Geoffrey?'

'Yes,' he says, 'and I'll tell you what I'll do. I'll swap you one of those pictures of Fred there for one of my hundred hundred plates.'

When Boycs completed his 100th first-class century for Yorkshire, a limited number of commemorative Coalport plates were made to mark the achievement. An artist's sketch of his face is at the heart of a wagon wheel of 100 spokes detailing each innings from 1963 to 1985.

'Deal,' I said.

So we arranged for the next Test match to be the handover ceremony. He gets Fred in full flow, and I get the porcelain which now has pride of place on display in my cottage in Yorkshire. Quietly, I was very pleased about this exchange from the off because this is a piece of cricket memorabilia featuring one of the best players that ever played for England. A true master of his craft. As a fellow opening batsman you had to admire his application and determination and the skill that allowed him to be so successful over such an extended period of time.

As Boycs walks off with Fred tucked under his arm, sporting that trademark grin of his, he's clearly happy too.

But he checks his strike and, unable to suppress his vanity, turns on his heels and says: 'You'll notice there are only a hundred on there. I got another fifty-one all told, you know!'

It was Boycott all over, that.

So proud was he of his personal achievements, particularly reaching the century of centuries, that he hosted a 40th anniversary dinner in honour of it in August 2017. Which made the wind-up played upon him the previous month by Jonathan Agnew, with the help of the *Test Match Special* statistician Andrew Samson, all the more brilliant.

Live on air during the Test match between England and South Africa at The Oval, Aggers persuasively informed the listeners of some breaking news, with Geoffrey alongside him in the summariser's seat. Between Toby Roland-Jones's deliveries to Dean Elgar in the fourth innings, he reads from a sheet of paper in front of him, allegedly distributed by Sami-ul-Hasan, the International Cricket Council's media manager, and carrying the ICC's official logo.

'Further from the recent request from the South African government,' Aggers began, 'the ICC has now considered the question of downgrading the status of all statistics, including runs and wickets, from the series played between England and the Rest of the World in 1970. The ICC agrees that the series was played against the spirit of the Gleneagles Agreement and, in the interests of keeping cricket free from political interference, all matches will be removed from first-class records. David Richardson, chief executive, says: "Clearly, this will not prove popular with those cricketers whose records will now be amended, but we are looking at the bigger picture.'''

Boycott's initial reaction during this wonderful 10-minute window was 'a load of tripe' and he quickly followed up with 'it's politics to interfere with it'.

As someone with a meticulous recollection of all his major performances, Boycs clearly knew the significance this had on his record but was trying to stay cool as Agnew probed away in a performance of greater precision than anything he managed as a seam bowler with Leicestershire. 'It's nothing to do with me personally but to say it's not first-class is nonsense,' Boycott insisted as Samson joins in with his statistical knowledge.

Acting as if the thoughts are popping into his head spontaneously, Samson referenced the 165-run stand between the ROW's captain Garfield Sobers and Graeme Pollock and Eddie Barlow's four wickets in five balls therefore being lost to the annals.

When asked directly if this would come in with immediate effect, Samson replied: 'We will have to see what the Association of Cricket Statisticians say.'

Our Geoffrey has already confirmed he played in the final two matches of a series that originally carried Test status before it was later revoked when he picks up the press release and reads out Sami's name, seemingly satisfied with the authenticity of the correspondence.

And then the *pièce de résistance* from Samson, who pointed out that Boycott's Headingley hundred would no longer be recognised as the site of his landmark 100th but his 99th such career score due to the one in the England v ROW series being expunged from the first-class records.

It was hilarious as Aggers then suggested the commemorative evening for 180 guests up at the Boycott residence near Wetherby in West Yorkshire would have to be canned and the others pressed him for the location of his true 100th hundred. Of course, he knew it was Faisalabad, Pakistan, later in the same year.

'It's a mess, an absolute mess,' Boycs suggested, as they continued their debate on the subject of statistics being altered as a result of the decision.

'It's also a complete wind-up, Geoffrey,' Aggers confirmed, as he removed his headset and vacated the commentator's chair.

'Is that right? You muppet, Agnew. I'll get you for that. You've done me a few times but that's the biggest one.'

Hook, line and sinker, I think you will agree. That joke is arguably the best I have heard on air because it was so prolonged and really played on Boycott's pride.

Normally Boycott has the last word in this kind of exchange, such as when Agnew commented on a TV camera shot of two Lord's members slumbering.

'They must have been watching videos of you batting, Geoffrey,' he said.

'Aye, they might have ... but when they wake up, I'll still be in!'

You have to acknowledge that is sharp. Certainly a lot sharper than in 2012 when England lost to South Africa at Lord's and the *Test Match Special* team welcomed Alice Cooper as their lunchtime guest. This slot always features an interesting person from another sphere, usually the world of entertainment, maybe from film, television or the theatre, in addition to a good number from music.

It would usually be someone who had a connection to the teams playing – for example, during an Ashes series you might have actors like Hugh Jackman and Russell Crowe pop in – or just a celebrity with a deep love of cricket. Every now and again they get a rock star. Think back to people like Brian May from Queen, Tom Chaplin from Keane or Harry Judd, the drummer from McFly.

On this occasion, however, they had got Alice in, which was quite extraordinary because he's an American, with no connection to the game. He grew up in Detroit watching baseball but he was in the UK, having headlined the Bloodstock heavy metal festival the previous weekend.

His image certainly didn't seem to fit with the BBC, but Jonathan Agnew had done his research and in came Alice with his manager Shep Gordon and his wife Sheryl Goddard.

Boycs has gone for lunch between the end of the morning session and the arrival of this rock entourage and returns just as the interview has been wound up. As he enters the commentary box. Aggers says to him: 'Geoffrey, you're just in time. Can I introduce you to Alice Cooper?'

To those that know their rock music, Alice Cooper has a rather sallow complexion, eyes sunk into the back of his head, and his mass of black hair hangs down long and lank.

With that, Boycs, turns to Sheryl, Cooper's missus, and says: 'Pleased to meet you, love.'

CHAPTER 6

The County Scene

The break-up of that great Yorkshire team coincided with prizes being distributed elsewhere around the shires. Take players of the quality of Fred Trueman, Ray Illingworth, Brian Close, Jimmy Binks and Ken Taylor out of any squad and it would be weakened.

County cricket became a buyer's market, arguably because of Brian Sellers, whose attitude towards Illingworth had been 'go, and take any other bugger with you'. There had been other clubs knocking on the door, and Worcestershire pushed through it with back-to-back titles in 1964 and 1965, between runners-up finishes in 1962 and 1966.

Another team that featured regularly at the business end during this decade was Glamorgan: second in 1963 and third in both 1966 and 1968. Although others came to the fore and they possessed some wonderful performers, it was one man that made this team special for me.

Don Shepherd was among my favourite guys to have

competed against and in my opinion the greatest player not to play international cricket for England. Just look at his record: 2,218 first-class wickets, the most by anyone without featuring in a Test match.

Shepherd converted to an off-spinner from a seamer in 1955, during his sixth season in first-class cricket, but to me when it came to bowling he was more of a cutter than an out-and-out spinner and devastating on uncovered pitches, particularly so with wicketkeepers of the quality of Eifion Jones and Dai Evans, who would later become an umpire. And great catchers around the bat.

In Peter Walker, Shepherd was aided by the best short leg of his and many another generation. Walker – who 'never wore a box, let alone all the armour they put on these days', Shepherd would later say – accounted for over 200 of his career dismissals and took in excess of 50 catches in each of the 1960 and 1961 seasons. Glamorgan were noted for their close fielding and in addition to Walker they also had Roger Davis, who would get into some dangerously close positions to sniff out chances; he once had to be resuscitated and later operated on to repair a fractured skull after being struck by a Neale Abberley leg glance in a match against Warwickshire in Cardiff.

Generally, the fielders had confidence in Shep because few batsmen could hit him. His career economy rate was just 2.14 and so he would just control a game. They used to say that Derek Underwood was unplayable in certain conditions. So was Shepherd, and he had the sort of pace that was perfect for the pitches of the day. He would be hitting them at the optimum kind of speed for the ball to grip and jag one way or t'other.

He certainly wasn't a flight bowler, one of those who would get it above your eyeline, instead landing these cutters with deadly accuracy. He was proud of the miserly economy rate that went with such an approach. Number one he would be thinking 'You're not going to score any runs,' and number two, 'Yeah, I'm going to get you out.'

He had a bit of a successor at Glamorgan in Steve 'Basil' Barwick. That sort of bowler was a pain in the backside for a batsman because you couldn't get after him, bowling the kind of length that introduced risk for attacking strokes and at a pace of about 65–70 mph. Quick enough for you to rule out using your feet to get down the pitch and change the dynamic.

As a batsman, he had you asking: 'Where am I going to score?' There was a tight in-field, placed perfectly after years of practice. As I mentioned, the close catchers would absolutely be in your pocket, too, because they had such confidence in Don pinning batsmen down and having the upper hand on any surface that offered even the slightest hint of seam movement.

Even the great players of the era couldn't get at him. The Australians of 1964 left Swansea to the echoes of patriotic song from the home support and a scorecard that not only revealed a defeat but showed Shepherd's miserly menace. He had taken match figures of nine for 93 from 69 overs. At times, he was in that category reserved only for the very best – unplayable.

So why didn't he play for England, then? Well, just look at his competition. It was competition indeed. He was up against Jim Laker, one of the very best off-spinners in history, and Tony Lock, the prolific slow left-armer, as well as the indefatigable Fred Titmus.

And being more of a cutter than a spinner, and therefore viewed as a bit of a British conditions specialist, you wouldn't have taken him abroad.

Of course, there were others who would come into that category of not making a play for international selection, despite phenomenal records in the Championship. We had one in Peter Lee at Lancashire during my days as captain. He would never get near England, never. But look at his wicket-taking capacity and you would wonder why on numbers alone. He took 100 wickets twice in three seasons, but he wouldn't get in because John Snow, Mike Hendrick, Chris Old, Bob Willis, Geoff Arnold and John Lever were all around. In that era, in the conditions that they were operating in, that lot were devastating. All had different facets to their bowling but the one word that you can say covered all of them was 'accurate', and if there was anything in the pitch they would find it and use it.

Perhaps Shepherd's batting went against him as well when it came to higher honours, or the lack of them. Although he once blitzed a half-century in a quarter of an hour against the touring Australians, his record of 156 first-class ducks will be hard to beat. Not many get the chance to bat that many times these days, whereas 1960s Championship cricket provided three seasons of 32 matches per team and half a dozen of 28.

So there would have been Welshmen wondering if they were set for an ignominious low when, in August 1971, Shepherd found himself striding to the crease at Grace Road with Glamorgan 11 for eight – one run shy of the lowest ever total in first-class matches between two counties, made by Northamptonshire against Gloucestershire in Gloucester in 1907.

The question he posed to his partner Peter Walker as he arrived in the middle suggested he knew what was at stake: 'Shall I get out and make history, or hang about and make a couple?' The couple he did contribute were undefeated but Glamorgan were dismissed for 24.

You could never doubt his commitment. Instead of travelling overseas on national service in winter months, Don pitched in to help with the running of the family-owned general store Shepherds in Parkmill, down on the Gower Peninsula.

I got to know him better at another one of his jobs later in life, as a broadcaster, through his great mucker Eddie Bevan. The two of them were Glamorgan cricket through and through and fabulous on the radio. Number one, they possessed great voices; that lovely shared lilt made them very listenable. Number two, they were unbelievably knowledgeable about Welsh cricket. Don through his cricket prowess; Edward from his journalistic background. They were certainly two during the 1980s and '90s – and I'd like to think that it goes on now – who would be sought out by players, by umpires, and other media colleagues at the end of a day's play to have a pint, and just talk cricket. Of how the game should be, and how it shouldn't.

As a bloke Don was absolutely brilliant company. A no-nonsense sort, he didn't suffer fools gladly. Which was rather like his approach to bowling. If you'd asked batsmen who was the one that they really didn't want to face during the 1960s he would be right up there. From 1960 to 1969 he took 1,014 wickets and despite his lack of pace he would have frightened opponents to death.

There were two other bowlers in county cricket during this era who dominated with a shared style of bowling. A very distinct style. What the *Playfair Cricket Annual* would list as 'medium'. Not medium-fast or fast-medium or fast. A distinctly different speed lower down the dial. Yes, bowlers of increased intensity would look to do something similar with the ball to get it challenging the edges of the bat but not with such deliberation. The two I am referring to are Tom Cartwright and Derek Shackleton. Like Shepherd, they would simply wear you down, wait for you to make a mistake, and allow movement off the pitch and bounce to contribute to your downfall. Unlike Shepherd, they were selected by England.

So why have we seen the widespread loss of this art when it comes to bowling? The answer is pitches. Wherever you went around the 17 counties at that time, each pitch would be different because you'd be playing mainly on the natural soil of that area. It was only in the late 1960s that they started introducing loam – a soil mix of sand, silt and clay – universally. As a result, pitches lost their idiosyncrasies and undoubtedly dissuaded bowlers to be different. When you got uncovered run-ups as well, it encouraged medium-pacers to trundle rather than tear-arse into the crease as you couldn't always be sure of your footing. From 1971, once a County Championship match began there would be no covering of the pitch at any time, and only much later did approaches to the crease get covered properly.

From 1968 to 1976, nine different counties won the title and it was Glamorgan's turn in 1969. Captained by Ossie Wheatley, they were a bloody good side, with batters of the ilk of Alan Jones, scorer of 35,000 first-class runs, at the top of the order, and Shepherd as the conductor of the bowling attack, setting the tune for the others. He would be supported on occasions by the sheer speed of Jeff Jones, although he tended to play more abroad for England than he would for Glamorgan, and Tony Cordle, the West Indies fast bowler who was the club's first overseas signing. It was a notable achievement to not only finish top but remain unbeaten.

There was the smell of success in the East Midlands, too, as I mentioned in the previous chapter. It wasn't necessarily sweet, however. Leicestershire were stocked to the brim with finger spinners. There were the offies in Ray Illingworth and Jack Birkenshaw and three slow left-armers in Tony Lock, who captained them to third in his final season of 1967, followed by John Steele and Chris Balderstone. Friars' Balsam would have done a roaring trade in the city of Leicester, I would have thought. The stuff had a real whiff to it, too.

Spinners used to dip their fingers into this ointment as it was supposed to harden the contact point of their spinning fingers. They called it the 'seg'. Some swore by this method. And sported brown fingers for their trouble. Others went a step further, believing that everything should be natural. No creams or solutions for them. They would just piss on their own hands. Or wee in a jar and pickle their digits that way. You always had to remember not to shake hands under any circumstances with the opposition when you went to Grace Road and under no circumstances accept sandwiches off them at tea either.

The 1960s and '70s were my formative years in the game and you would come up against some real characters. Brian Bolus being one. Later in my career, as England coach, I came across Brian again and I was disappointed with him. He was on the ill-fated EMAC – the England Management Advisory Committee – chaired by Bob Bennett and also including David Acfield and Doug Insole. Brian was also a selector and I felt he was trying to undermine me at that time.

During his playing days, when he moved from Yorkshire to Nottinghamshire and represented England, I had been rather fond of him. He was one of those eccentric cricketers who proved a magnet for fun. An accumulator of runs, Bolus attracted as much attention when the ball struck his legs as when it struck his bat.

That was because he was famed for wearing these enormous pads. His front one looked like a mattress from front on, and in an era in which umpires would not give you out when you were struck on the front foot, he used to kick it – and I mean kick it – in the knowledge he wouldn't be out. As his pad was bolstered, there was no pain to his method.

Bolus had an opening partner at Nottinghamshire called Norman Hill, who was quite an ample chap. Quite a size indeed. Just think of Colin Milburn, that carefree colossus whose ball-striking ability won him four Test caps but whose immobility cost him his England place. They were both roly-poly guys.

At Old Trafford, in one of my early games for Lancashire in the 1966 season, Bolus and Hill had us in stitches with their running between the wickets. These days, boundaries for Championship cricket can be ludicrously short. Back then, we would play on the entire surface. There would be no cushions 25 yards in for us to land on after a chase to the boundary, preventing us from sliding into advertising boards. There was no rope at all, and if a batsman wanted to hit a four he would have to strike the ball all the way to the perimeter fence.

And so on the occasion in question, the game is just past the halfway point, courtesy of a Lancashire declaration 47 runs ahead on first innings, and Bolus has hit Brian Statham, our captain, into the distance while still in arrears. It was obvious on this size ground that the batsmen would have to run hard every time the ball was struck beyond the infield and Bolus and his regular opening partner Hill, whose nickname, fittingly, was 'Nimble', had a dialogue for such eventualities.

The ball was travelling into the deep midwicket region towards the only covered stand we had in Manchester at that time, known simply as H Stand.

'There's plenty there, Nimble.'

To which came the reply: 'Think there are several, Bolly.'

As the ball is some hundred or so yards away, there is plenty of scope for this chat between the pair to develop further.

'There's another one there, Nimble.'

'Yes, I'm right with you, Bolly.'

Only he wasn't. He was run out, diving in a heap in a forlorn attempt to make his ground, going for the fifth run! Hauling himself to his feet, he went off, wheezing and coughing, not taking too kindly to the uncharacteristic exertions.

It would no doubt have raised a chortle from Draught Bass Harry, the infamous supporter housed in H Stand who supped a pint every time a Lancashire wicket went down. On several occasions, the opposition would have us 90 for eight at lunchtime and he would be shouting and bawling and carrying on to the point where he would be led out of the ground just after one o'clock. He must have enjoyed us taking the odd wicket, too.

Bolus was also an opponent in the weird weather game in the midsummer of 1975 when, in bright sunshine, a Lancashire team I was captain of piled up 477 for five declared on day one and had taken two home wickets by the close. Ice creams and sun cream were the order of the day at Buxton, one of the highest if not *the* highest town in England. This was one of the hottest summers on record, yet on the Monday, the scheduled second day's play following a Sunday hiatus for a one-day match elsewhere, not a ball was possible. The ground was initially soaked with rain and then covered by thick snow. On the second day of June!

Such circumstances were made for Dickie Bird as umpire. The frozen nature of the ground made it unplayable on that Monday but when the sun came out and thawed things on the

Tuesday, he and his partner Dusty Rhodes deemed it ready for a resumption. Due to the drastic changes in the elements, steam was coming off it when play resumed.

This was a game of strange occurrences, though, also featuring the moment that the Derbyshire all-rounder Ashley Harvey-Walker took his false teeth out, wrapped them in a handkerchief and gave them to Dickie at the start of one of his bowling spells.

As we left a ground painted white the afternoon before, there had been scant chance of a result without some creativity, it seemed, but we bowled Derbyshire out for 42 in the first innings, which gave me the opportunity to knock on the home dressing-room door to tell Bob Taylor, my opposite number as captain, that faced with a 435-run deficit on first innings, I would like them to bat again.

'Thank you very much,' came the reply from Bolus, who would be tasked with getting back out there to face the new ball on a thawing seamer. 'I can feel a desperate innings coming on again!'

As a player he was a bloody good character and one who always gave you a chuckle. One of those that made the county game so much fun to be a part of. A character unafraid to do things his own way. To be different.

That included one of the strangest pre-match practice rituals I have come across. As a county captain he put a lot of pressure on himself to win the toss, believing it was key to setting the agenda in a three-day match. It can be, of course. If it's a bit dank and there is a touch of morning sizzle in late April, you want a bowl. If it's cracking the flags in August and you have two spinners in your team, then it's bat first and rack 'em up. And so, as one would when it comes to batting or bowling, he used to work on his technique pre-match. Yes, he would be in the dressing room, practising tossing.

And to make things as authentic as he possibly could, he did so using a green towel, believing that it was necessary to re-create something that at least looked like the pitch for the coin to land upon, methodically going through, getting one of his teammates to write down for the record his success rate behind closed doors. First, he would toss and allow others to call. Then vice versa. Of course, if he was on a decent run in the sanctity of the dressing room you could bet your bottom dollar he would then promptly get out to the middle and lose!

His attention to detail for the traditional practice of coin tossing was certainly not shared by Sir Ian Botham. No: there was none of this business of putting the club blazer on, or getting out to the middle to shake hands on the eve of a match when Beefy was in charge. In fact, after a very heavy night, he used to toss up on the balcony at Taunton if his opposing captain agreed. If he won the right to choose, he didn't even look at what the pitch was like; he would respond with: 'We will bat.' And then he would lie down with a pork pie for company. Within five minutes of devouring it, he would be asleep.

Beefy had a long-lasting relationship with said meat products. To his very last Test as a Sky Sports commentator, during the 2019 Ashes, he still got half a dozen of these Melton Mowbray pies made by Dickinson & Morris delivered to every match.

Now that he's retired, I can declare that I used to pinch one and take it down to my colleagues in the press box. If he knew that I was giving a slice to Charlie Sale, of the *Daily Mail*, he would have strung me up. Sale, my former colleague and writer of the hard-hitting Sports Agenda column, left no stone unturned to absolutely nail everybody he could, Beefy included.

Bolus was fun but he was trumped by Brian 'Tonker' Taylor, captain of an Essex team on the rise from the adversity of their club almost going to the wall. It was not until 1966 that Essex owned their own home in Chelmsford and only did so thanks in no small part to the Warwickshire Supporters' Association digging deep for the good of the wider game. It coincided with record losses and a cutting of the financial cloth that left just 13 players on the staff, but he somehow galvanised them.

Tonker had an interesting CV, which included 301 consecutive County Championship appearances and notoriety as one of the few men to be named Cricket Writers' Young Player of the Year and not be capped by England, although he did travel to South Africa in 1956–57 as Godfrey Evans's understudy. In retirement he became an England selector.

As a captain, he was a father figure to a side which included Brian Hardie, Brian Edmeades, Keith Fletcher, Raymond East, David Acfield, John Lever and Keith Pont. This lot were crackers and Tonker, so monikered for his aggressive approach to batting, would be entrusted to keep them all in check. And they loved him to bits, absolutely adored him.

As for his own playing credentials, with the bat he would

give it a thrash – he liked to pull and hook – but as a wicket-keeper it's fair to say he wore gloves for no apparent reason. During matches he would tell the left-arm spinner East: 'Just aim at these gloves, Raymond. Just aim at these gloves.' He was not a keeper that liked it spinning.

There is one fabulous story about him in a Benson & Hedges Cup semi-final in 1973. Essex are away against Kent and the St Lawrence Ground in Canterbury is packed. There is great anticipation of his team making a Lord's final and Tonker turns up with a brand-new pair of wicket-keeping gloves.

You have to remember that, in the era in question, you didn't just pull cricket equipment out of its cellophane and walk out into the middle as is the modern way. Gloves, like bats, had to be knocked in. They had to be worn, manipulated so that they lost their stiffness and felt moulded to your own hands.

On this occasion, however – and quite a grand occasion at that, as I have mentioned – he whipped them straight out of the packet and asked for help from teammates to shove them on as there was absolutely no bend in them at all.

Now, Tonker possessed a bit of a sergeant major's voice. A bit like Windsor Davies in *It Ain't Half Hot, Mum*. And he had this command about him to which his words might not do justice.

'Big occasion, special occasion this, new gloves. Gotta wear new gloves for a big occasion.'

He just wanted to look the part for a match of such magnitude – although during a period in which wicketkeepers wore pads up to their waists, this was easier said than done. Nevertheless, he walked out proud as punch, leading his team.

The first ball of the match from John Lever comes down, and it hits his gloves and drops straight to the floor – his gloves have not cupped at all. The rest of the team have tears in their eyes looking at it on the grass, where it's dropped in front of him. And, of course, he can't pick it up. There's just no give at all in these leather contraptions and it forced him into a bit of improvisation, placing one hand flat on the floor and, in a brush and shovel method, manoeuvred the ball onto it, offering it to first slip off what looked like a tray covered in rubber dimples.

Cue a temporary stoppage: 'Fink I better change these things,' he said, switching to his old 'uns.

Taylor was much older than most of his team but there was a genuine affection for him despite him being the butt of dressing-room banter. He was both loved as a senior mate and respected as a leader. Not one of the game's tactical geniuses, he would nevertheless be looking to put the metaphorical arm round his young charges' shoulders.

Talk of his masterplan to dismiss Yorkshire's Geoffrey Boycott in 1972 still brings chortles and draws tears to the eyes of those who played under him. That run machine Boycott had taken double hundreds off Essex's attack at Colchester in the previous two seasons and was naturally the danger man whenever Yorkshire were opponents. The difficulty was finding ways to get him out.

Of course, our Geoffrey's defensive game was par excellence, but he was a compulsive hooker, something Tonker felt he could exploit through the fast bowling of Essex's West Indies international Keith Boyce. So, to have Boyce in peak physical condition to deliver the top-speed bouncers he believed could account for Boycott's wicket, Taylor gave the overseas star the preceding match off.

'The quickest bumper you've ever bowled, Boycey, son,' Tonker ordered, after an initial instruction to pitch the first two up at half-throttle. The idea had been to get Boycs on the front foot, before delivering the *coup de grâce*.

This subtlety was supplemented by Tonker pushing another man back on the hook just as Boyce was running in for that all-important third ball, a move not strictly legal and one that caused all the hoo-ha between Mike Gatting and umpire Shakoor Rana in the infamous Faisalabad Test of 1987.

As expected, Boycott patted the first two balls back to mid-off, at which point the wink-wink-nudge-nudge routine went into action. Miraculously for a man who liked a late night, Boycey remembered his instructions. As Boycott shaped to hook, Tonker, from his vantage point behind the stumps, turned to the men set deep on the leg-side and bellowed: 'CATCH IT!!!'

Trouble was, Tonker had turned his eyes to where he thought the ball was headed and not to where it had actually gone, which was off Boycott's gloves and through to him, from where it quickly went to ground. Still, despite the fluff, the masterplan remained a minor triumph – Boycott only went on to make 121, and not one of the big double hundreds which had spawned the idea in the first place.

When Tonker retired from first-class cricket, he played

on for Essex's second XI, of which he was captain, and then moved to Cambridge, where he was the university's cricket coach. He simplified things for his younger teammates and bigged them up as if they were Bradmans-in-waiting while denigrating the opposition. He was a mentor, a father figure who, rather than crack the whip, would put his arm around his teammates. They loved him to bits and make no mistake: this is a team that were crackers.

Ray East was one of the funniest people I've ever come across on a cricket field. This is the lad who was famously given out caught behind by Arthur Jepson, the last ball before tea. As the players left the field, the scoreboard changed from six wickets down to seven.

Yet after tea, Raymond, with helmet on, took his place at the non-striker's end.

'All right, Arthur,' he said.

'Eee, aye, I give ye out,' Jepson said to him.

'What do you mean, you gave me out.'

'You were out . . .'

'Nah, nah. Didn't touch that. I wasn't out. I didn't see you give me out, Arthur.'

In another game at Chelmsford, the opposing batsmen were tanking him for fours and sixes and Essex went on to lose. Next game, once the opening bowlers had had their go and the medium-pacer Brian Edmeades had come on, it was time for spin.

'Positions for Raymond,' bellowed Tonker from behind the stumps.

Keith Pont walked out of the ground and stationed himself

on the bridge which spans the River Chelmer, waving his arms in the air because that's where he'd kept going the match before.

Pont was another who didn't take himself too seriously, and so came up with a comedic response to being asked to do a bit of third man to third man while fielding one day. I am not sure why Tonker placed him down there for both ends, as haring from one end of the outfield to the other is a real no-no. Pont eased the physical burden required, however, when he took on loan a kid's bicycle, unbeknownst to his captain, to make his way to the other end of the ground at the end of every over. Bloody crackers, they were.

Take an example in my retirement. Of course, it had to be Essex as one of the teams for my first game of a three-year spell as a first-class umpire. I'm nervous as it is at the start. And when I got the fixtures at the start of the season, my heart sunk. I thought: 'No!'

I was a new boy on the umpiring scene and awaiting me were lads I have had that much fun with over the years. It was Essex v Cambridge University at Fenner's and the visitors were bowling first. John Lever was about to bowl, and everything seemed fine. 'Play,' I said, and he ran up to the crease. Next thing, there was a massive explosion. WTF! He hadn't bowled a leather ball. He'd bowled an orange, and it had splattered everywhere.

I was stood with David Constant and I just let it pass, not saying dead ball or anything in the confusion, so it counted as one of the six deliveries for the first over.

On another occasion, myself and Lloyd Budd, who was

Bert Flack, Old Trafford groundsman. A real character, a very likeable chap but formidable.

The Don, chatting with Ray Bright with Rod Marsh looking on during the opening ceremony of the Centenary Test match between Australia and England in 1977.

A special time at Lord's winning the Gillette Cup in 1975. Clive Lloyd and Farokh Engineer were perfect signings for Lancashire. Two Great Men.

Brian Close. He wrote a book titled, *I Don't Bruise Easily*. He was in his element against the West Indies with their ferocious bowling attack, here in the third Test at Old Trafford in 1976.

I never cease to chuckle at this pic! Lillee and Miandad: both greats . . . and both up for a scrap!

A fellow Accringtonian, Graeme Fowler was my opening partner at Lancashire and my travelling companion. We loved a sing song in the car! He was a proper singer, too, having been in the Lancashire Youth Choir . . . think Phil Collins . . . Oh, and what a terrific batsman he was.

The Sky Crew celebrating Sky's 100th Live Test Match in 2006. Sky have been great to me. A brilliant production team down the years who make us at front of camera look good. (Back L-R: Michael Holding, David Gower; front L-R: Nasser Hussain, David Lloyd, Michael Atherton, Ian Botham.)

Three all-time greats . . . Pollock, Holding, Warne. Looks like Shane has had a good night!

Bob is sadly no longer with us. A great mate, a great bloke, all of us will miss him terribly. A quite brilliant broadcaster, unique in the way that he could split an audience. And a night out with Bob, or indeed an 'all-dayer' was very memorable . . . if only you could remember!

Pipes of Peace . . . Flintoff with teammates Neil Fairbrother, Ian Austin, Darren Gough and physio Wayne Morton . . . me too!

Last of the Summer Wine with Allott and Atherton . . . of course, I had to be Compo.

Me 'n' Athers in St Lucia. Nowt better than a rum shack.

A memorable golf day at Mere Golf and Country Club with the lads from Phoenix Management. (Back L–R: Michael Lumb, Ben Stokes, Stuart Broad, Neil Fairbrother, David Lloyd; front L–R: Joe Root, Paul Collingwood.)

Hobbit . . . We did a Sky shoot in New Zealand where all the filming was done. Nasser was a wonderful captain for England and formed a great partnership with coach Duncan Fletcher. Now he is one of the best and most sought-after commentators in the business. A mate and a top man.

What a player! KP . . . this is the celebration for his hundred at The Oval in 2005, an innings that took my breath away.

Ashes (below) and World Cup 2019. It has to be Ben Stokes (with a little help from Jack Leach) at Headingley with a Bothamesque innings and then the World Cup Final at Lords. Both performances tell you that he is a modern Great . . . and a super lad, too.

The Big Two . . . Jimmy Anderson and Stuart Broad – England's best ever opening bowling partnership. Their discipline, attention to detail, skill, commitment, attitude, fitness, stamina . . . I could go on. Outstanding.

Now these pair are two of my favourite cricketers: Rash 'n' Mo. Diversity is important in our game and these two lads fly a very important flag for British Asians. I can tell you they are an absolute hoot as well!

Ed pops in now and again. He is *so* down to
earth . . . had to have a selfie!

Best pic I've ever had! All four were brilliant. Mick and Charlie will chat cricket,
Ronnie will be chasing after his young twins, and Keith . . . well he's just Keith . . .

a retired policeman, were rooming together. Ray East was second XI coach at Essex and also running a beautiful pub in East Bergholt called the Red Lion, so we stayed there. Ray had promised us a morning venture before a Sunday League match. A culture trip if you like.

'This is Constable country is this, John Constable,' he said. 'Flatford Mill, just up the road.'

Indeed, *Flatford Mill (Scene on a Navigable River)* depicts a working rural scene from just over the county border in Suffolk as two lighter barges and their crew progress up the River Stour from Dedham Lock.

'We'll go. I'll show you.'

So there was this National Trust house at Flatford. Easty knocked on the door and this caretaker-type bloke opened it.

'Good morning. Is John in?' Easty asked.

'John?'

'John Constable. I've got some friends who would like to meet him.'

'I'm afraid he's dead, sir.'

'Dead? When did he die?'

Budd and I were absolutely beside ourselves with laughter. He was a sandwich short, Easty, but wonderful company.

With such mischievous characters on the field, county cricket needed guardians to keep it in check and it was reflected in the sort of captains found around the shires in the 1970s. In addition to Tonker – such an affectionate bloke who would genuinely always want you to do well, even as an opponent – there were other father figure-style captains like Tony Brown of Gloucestershire and Wheatley at Glamorgan.

Blokes who were usually elder statesmen, who'd done it all. Of course, the professional nature of the game now means that these kinds of appointments are a thing of a bygone era.

As in the model at Essex, it was not unusual for the captain/ senior pro to take on the leadership or management of the second XI when they finished up. They might even take the second XI captaincy on for a season or two to help mentor those pushing for a place in the first team. These were the guys who effectively ran a county's production line and enforced a code of conduct for the way the club would be represented, ensuring that the game was played in a proper way.

And here's something just to dwell on in an age when player behaviour in international cricket has been under such scrutiny. As a player in the 1960s and '70s, if you did something out of line the opposition captain would talk to your captain. Perhaps say, 'You need to keep an eye on this young chap.' And then your captain would 'pull you' – a bit like a headmaster might, which sounds rather draconian – to remind you how to behave. So, for example, if as a bats- man you gave the impression that you were questioning an umpire's decision, there would be a comeback and you wouldn't be allowed to do it again. It was no big deal, just a way of learning the respect required for professional cricket, and might include a request from your captain to go and knock on the door of the umpire and say: 'Excuse me, can I just apologise for my conduct today?'

After Tonker's reign, Keith Fletcher came in and tried to straighten Essex up. They were a very good team, and would transform from nearly men to perennial winners by the end of the 1970s, while maintaining their game-for-a-laugh attitude. It is hard to quantify in this day and age, but having a good time was part of their make-up; the way they played. They would lure you in by taking the piss from morning till night, but they could play, and if you couldn't combine the fun element with the serious aspect of competitive cricket then they would be all over you.

There was Graham Gooch coming through at that time, Keith Boyce, Norbert Phillip – two tasty, tasty fast bowlers. Someone like Derek Pringle would have been weaned on Tonker's enthusiasm and Fletcher's pragmatism in pursuit of wins.

Fletch was a good colleague of mine for England, a brilliant county captain and someone who also coached England. He possessed a great cricket mind and was a godsend for young players – just ask Nasser Hussain. He would look after them, in the same mould as Taylor really, improving them, showing them the right way. So he pulled Nasser every now and again about being a bit naughty.

Generally, although Fletch still gave them their head, he tried to get away from this flipping nuthouse team environment fostered in Taylor's time. The big difference I saw from outside of it was that they knew when to rein it in under Fletch. He would pull them all together. Because his one important characteristic – and he didn't always look that way, often giving the impression that he wasn't – was that he was quite steely. A no-nonsense kind of guy. He might have been compared to an amiable gnome over the years but don't let his nickname fool you.

Essex became a force, a real, real force in County Championship cricket, finishing second in 1978 and being crowned champions the following year and in 1983, 1984 and 1986. During an era in which matches had to be regularly set up with declarations and forfeitures in the pursuit of positive results, it was quite a skill to continually lure teams in with negotiation and then get the better of them on the field.

Fletcher was hell-bent on winning that first Championship, and his attitude towards maximising play highlighted it. A fixture list of 22 matches – the decade had started with 24 but it had been reduced to 20 between 1972 and 1976 to accommodate one-day competitions – meant that when it rained, it produced natural time off and you rested. There would be a game of cards, or one or two would do the crossword.

Not Fletch. He was a weather watcher. Always in the umpires' ears: 'Get us on.' He would tell them: 'We can't get any points sat watching this lot fall from above, get us on, and we'll play. We'll play in anything. Just get us on that field.'

Remember, with travel days filling the gaps between the 66 scheduled days of cricket, umpires liked a bit of time off as well so he had to be persuasive, but on the flip side he was one of the few who would argue to bin a football warm-up to get back into the middle a quarter of an hour earlier.

'You can't take points sat in that dressing room,' was Fletcher's philosophy. He would chivvy them along, knowing that there would be rain in other parts of the country. The thought of getting onto the field ahead of rivals only spurred him on in campaigning further.

A couple of extra points here and there, and a win when everybody else was rained off. That's an example of how you might get one step ahead in the quest for success. Championship pennants were decided not by restricting losses but maximising wins and a good crop would be contrived ones. If a stalemate ensued, you would try to come to an arrangement whereby there would be a fourth innings against the clock.

A kind of scenario that would result in a negotiation of 'We'll leave you this target, if you give us so many overs to bowl'. You were ensuring that you got a game of cricket by manipulating it. There might be some lob bowling introduced to boost the opposition score and manufacture a game within a game. It was not knowingly altering the odds, nothing like fixing and spot-fixing. It was fixing a game situation but was nothing like skulduggery. No, what we were doing was setting up a meaningful match in the absence of one developing via natural methods. And in broad sight.

Of course, Fletch was a shrewd operator. It was said that he would sit down at the start of every season and map out where across the 22 fixtures the victories could be accrued. It would take a dozen or so for a team to come out on top and some captains, naturally enough, would not want to get into a transaction with a wheeler-dealer like him, preferring the cautious approach of not losing rather than risking a share of the game for a win. Generally, he would also ask his players to take risks for the greater good. To not worry about their individual averages but the team cause.

His persuasive powers never worked on the likes

of Worcestershire's Phil Neale or Norman Gifford, of Warwickshire, and the umpires looked less favourably on his appeal than that of opposing captain Ian Botham when, during the 1985 season, heavy rain fell ahead of the second day at Taunton. Having crashed a big hundred on day one, Beefy did not fancy hanging about for Fletcher time – a couple of hours in the evening in which the Essex man would be making his case to get on. The Botham counter-argument would be for a gathering in the now-defunct Four Alls pub or playing a round of golf. History will tell you that there was no play on the second day of that match.

Pub trips were a feature of away games versus Somerset. Fred Rumsey, a big, burly left-arm opening bowler who could get it down with good wheels, was a fabulous host, taking us to the Angel Hotel, on Corporation Street, a couple of hundred yards' walk to the ground. Back in the day it had a skittle alley. A proper one in which you had to set the skittles back up yourself. Not like the modern 10-pin versions which are lifted into place by robots. And you would have to fetch your ball back, too. And so it would be beer and skittles as pre-match entertainment.

On one particular trip down to the South-west, during Brian Statham's time as captain, we had with us wicketkeeper Keith Goodwin, a man who was a terror. I used to be frightened to death of him. Goody had been in the army and wasn't shy in letting others know 'I've killed a man'.

Fred met us, drink was taken, and everybody was merry enough until Goody started singing one of his dirges. The rest of us knew well enough not to interrupt as the usual response was a stern look and a reminder from Goody: 'One singer, one song.'

He would then proceed with this sad tale about the demise of Patrick McCaffery, triggered by a simple failure to fulfil a menial set of orders from his army captain.

Only Fred wasn't having this, and, annoyed that the conversation had been stopped stone dead at a time when he had popped down to see friends and socialise, kicked off about it. Next thing, Fred and Goody have squared up to each other.

Now this is a real catchweight contest because Goodwin was quite a squat, little bloke and Fred was big, standing well over six foot. So they squared up with their dukes out, at which point Fred picked Goody up and squeezed the air out of him with a huge bear hug.

Unfortunately, that wasn't the end of things though. Goodwin's face was now right in front of Fred's as a result and so he bit his nose! Fred dropped him like a stone, and the evening ended abruptly with Rumsey holding his hooter. Next morning, he opened the bowling sporting a large Elastoplast.

Fred enjoyed a scrumpy cider or two and on a hot day became a rather thirsty chap. On one occasion I recall him having a pint of scrumpy down on the boundary, and throwing his sweater onto the turf next to it. Some dog then wandered over and pissed on it.

Hail-fellow-well-met was Fred, always the most sociable of opponents, and was, most importantly, a champion of players as a founder of the players' union – the Professional Cricketers' Association. During the late 1960s, at the start of the professional era, everybody was frightened to death of being sacked by their club for attending union meetings.

But he was adamant that English county cricketers should be paid and treated better and so he, Jack Bannister and John Arlott toughed it out despite the threat of retribution from the committee men they were taking on. The PCA membership owes so much to those blokes. Not just the 40 or so that attended that first gathering, including myself, but all those who have followed in their footsteps. Before this intervention players had such poor rights in relation to their employers and improved contracts made them less subservient to committees made up of amateurs.

As an entrepreneur, Fred ran his own travel company and was involved in several other businesses, his eye for a profit serving him well.

He was also a fine new-ball bowler. A real blood-and-guts competitor who gave it everything, his bowling was all about pace, and he was once clocked at 93 mph by one of the game's early speed guns. He was one of those who absolutely charged in during a career of 580 first-class wickets at an outstanding 20.29 runs apiece. Only Keith Boyce and Joel Garner bettered his List A bowling average of 16.8 and no one of any standing could cut in below his economy rate of just 2.73.

He made five Test appearances for England, making his debut in the high-scoring Ashes game at Old Trafford in 1964 when Bobby Simpson got 311. Brian Statham and Fred Trueman did not play, the latter left out despite England trailing 1-0 with two matches to play, due to a featherbed pitch in Manchester and a stiff difference of opinion with Ted

Dexter, the captain. It meant Rumsey and Tom Cartwright were handed a baptism of fire instead.

The two Freds did bowl together very briefly late in their careers, however, as Derbyshire teammates in the John Player League every Sunday, but it was when he was bounding around, or hosting, under the Quantocks that this prodigious philanthropist really shone.

CHAPTER 7

The Imports

During the majority of my playing career every county had at least a couple of crackerjack players from abroad. County cricket was awash with the world's richest talent.

These were players who would more than hold their own in the most elevated company. Turn up at Bristol and there would be the South African all-rounder Mike Procter and Zaheer Abbas, that silkiest of batsmen from Pakistan, in the Gloucestershire XI. Hampshire had Barry Richards and Andy Roberts, then later paired Gordon Greenidge with Malcolm Marshall. Talk about Caribbean flair. In addition to a certain Ian Terence Botham, Somerset had cricketing royalty in Sir Vivian Richards and Joel Garner.

Richards was always generous with his time and willing to have a yarn about the game, but his biggest contribution to cricket for me was as an opponent. When you played against this champion batsman you felt inspired. He was such a fine player to watch, in fact, that you actually wanted him to get a few runs. Not too many, mind, just enough to enjoy his array of outrageous shots.

There is a trait shared by all the great players throughout history: bravery. They are frightened of nothing. Viv exemplified this not only in the way he played the game but in his mannerisms, showing witnesses the confidence he felt when he entered the field. I used to say to people, 'I wish I could walk like that,' relating to the strut he would indulge in on his way to the crease. His entrance was gladiatorial. In modern terms it was like a boxer's walk to the ring. And he lapped it all up like a prizefighter, too, loving the fact that there would be a real buzz as he approached the wicket.

Very few in history genuinely got you on the edge of your seat. But Viv was one, and in this regard I would compare him to Kevin Pietersen, the best England player I've ever seen, or Brian Lara, another box-office batter from the Caribbean.

Viv would tell you that he would lose form like everybody else. He was also someone who, despite being renowned for his aggression, was very big on defensive play and the art of it. To make sure all his other shots were in order, he knew his defence had to be right. It is at the heart of a batsman's game. Other guys, even some of the world's leading players, made the mistake of still going hard at the ball when they were defending, trying to push through the line. But that invited danger because the firmer a push, the greater distance an edge would carry. He would argue that when playing defensively, you should be looking to drop the ball dead at your feet.

It might surprise people who remember him as this

fabulous, carefree stroke-maker that when he wanted to be technical, he could be technical. He said technique developed from when you were looking to defend – because you need to be quite precise about it. But when he was on the attack he prepared his mind for being exactly that – attacking. He was good at separating the two.

He reckoned that when he was in good nick the ball looked enormous. Equally it would reduce in size during the times he felt out of it. The key, he said, was to try to eliminate the things that had led you to fail in the past, and remember the things that made you successful. That it felt quite special when you were able to get that balance right of throwing things out of the door that were not necessary, and retaining those things that would help you accomplish what you wanted to achieve.

He was an intimidating batsman to bowl at and the stumps looked tiny when he was stood in front of them. Many a bowler would tell you that. If you targeted them he would more often than not whip you over the leg-side for four or six.

Because of the way he played, your first thought in trying to get him out would be lbw. So you had to get the ball full and rely on the fact that he might miss one early, as any batsman can. The problem was he was so accomplished at working the ball from anywhere within his reach to the on-side with minimum effort. He would play huge shots and there is nothing more thrilling than seeing someone play the hook – especially when that someone is not wearing a helmet.

We can all appreciate the risk involved there and the precision with which that stroke has to be played to avoid injury. To his great credit, Viv never used to miss it. His eye was as good as anybody's but like all of us the ageing process inevitably means that sight and therefore reactions wane. So later in his career, when he was finishing off at Glamorgan, he had to work a lot harder.

But I recall a game at Southport in 1977 between Lancashire and Somerset when he was in his mid twenties and we decided to test out those reactions. Colin Croft, our West Indies fast bowler, tested him with some bouncers in the first innings of the match. Richards' response to one of them was to hit it into the railway line. Us mere mortals would have been ducking out of the way and hoping the ball missed us. But he pummelled it miles. His innings of 189 came in a Somerset scorecard of 308 all out. The next best innings was 31. He made it look like he was playing a different game from everyone else. Viv could also pull off the front foot and that showed you the time he had in playing cross-bat shots – he could rock forward and still adjust rather than having to go fully back.

He was that good, he toyed with people. I remember umpiring a game at Taunton in 1986 when Viv brought up three figures off just 48 balls against Glamorgan, an innings that saw him win the Walter Lawrence Trophy for the season's fastest hundred. And he had not made contact with his first few deliveries, either. Until that is, the visiting fast bowler Greg Thomas provoked a reaction.

After beating the great man a few times in an over, the England international Thomas said: 'Hey, Viv, it's round, it's red and it weighs five ounces. Now try playing it!'

With those words, the beast had been unleashed. Viv

responded by smashing the ball out of the ground and saying to Thomas: 'You know what it looks like, now you go and find it!'

When stood at the non-striking end, Richards had a habit of knocking the top of his bat handle with the palm of his hand and had this sort of snort. He stood there, hammering away on his bat and grunting, I knew he was ticking. He was ferocious in this kind of mood.

It is not the biggest of grounds, straight towards the River Tone, and he said to me with a glint in his eye: 'Bumbles, look who coming on now – the Ontong.' (A reference to Glamorgan's captain, the off-spinner Rodney Ontong.) 'I hit him in the river.' And he did, regularly.

The likes of Richards are great for the game, pushing new boundaries and encouraging higher aspirations. He had such all-around talent: in addition to 114 first-class hundreds, he was a brilliant fielder, decent off-spinner and someone who off about four steps could wang the ball down at a decent pace when he wanted.

People wanted to be at games in which he played, which was emphasised in a one-day international between West Indies and England at Trent Bridge in 1984. Geoff Miller got Viv out for just three, something that was naturally a great source of pride yet caused him quite a bit of grief. At the end of the over of said dismissal, Dusty trekked down to third man expecting to take the applause of the crowd but received anything but from one particular bloke.

'Miller, you complete tosser, I've come to watch Viv Richards, not f***ing you!'

Viv was a memorable scalp. You were in awe of him,

admired him and aspired to be him. I bowled him for a single-figure score in the last game of the 1982 county season. In the first innings at Taunton it had been Lancashire 165; Richards 178. Despite a hefty first innings deficit, though, we went on to win the match by 14 runs. In the greater scheme of things it didn't matter very much, although it mattered to me!

That barracker from the stands in Nottingham was unfortunate in the extreme. The three-wicket Texaco Trophy win was a rare one for England over that great West Indies team and came just 48 hours after Richards had wowed Old Trafford with an incredible unbeaten 189. He also gave the Lord's crowd an exhibition in hitting an unbeaten 84, off just 65 balls, to seal a 2-1 series win.

English supporters were spoilt by the fact that he was over here playing county cricket every summer, too, and it's a great shame that we no longer have that class of player here annually. The various Twenty20 tournaments around the world have seen to that, with the world's best making them a priority over stints at county clubs.

As a player 40 or 50 years ago, you would look forward to coming up against the very best and we would get a chance to test ourselves against genuine legends of the sport like Richards, Imran Khan and Richard Hadlee. You would look forward to the battle, in the knowledge that these stars of the global game would be doing everything they could to help their adopted counties be successful. Spectators would go along just to watch these kinds of blokes and we would appreciate the chance of pitting our wits against them.

These days you get most overseas players jetting in and out for stints varying in length between three weeks and three months, and I feel that this is a flawed aspect of the county game. It takes time to get to know a teammate and modern players are missing out in my opinion because becoming part of the fabric of the domestic game here would improve them as cricketers for the good of their own countries.

Richards always believed that attitude played a huge part in the player he became. He was committed to playing without fear, and in believing in what he was doing. The fact that he came from a small Caribbean island also gave him the determination to go on to bigger and better things. If you talk to him, he attributes his Test debut in India in 1974 as the key milepost in his career. There were 70,000 people in Bangalore. Later in the series, 90,000 turned up in Calcutta. As he says, that was more people than live in Antigua – the size of its entire population being somewhere in between those two attendances.

Being able to impress that many people gave him the desire to succeed. Entertainers always like big crowds. Who wouldn't like that multitude turning up to watch them? He was committed to giving people a show that would live with them for a long time. And that was the thing about him. You remembered his innings – the poses he would get into at the crease, the dismissive nature of his stroke-making.

With Viv as their star turn, West Indies were able to put together a great team from all those Caribbean islands. And although people question the relationships, and tensions, between some of the different nations, they really came together well and assembled a unit. Collectively the players had a great spirit, and it sent a message of unity to the people of the West Indies.

For Viv, there was not only pride in representing them but in the fact that West Indies were indisputably top dogs. That Windies team during the 1980s were the best ever. They had a batting line-up to die for and a desire to play positive cricket. They were full of attacking intent, apart from Larry Gomes who was the glue that held the batting together at number three. His job would be to soak up the good balls and to get rid of the strike whenever he could.

As a bloke he could be aggressive, but I would argue that you need one or two with such characteristics in every successful team. Players that play on the front foot and give no quarter when it comes to a direct contest between bat and ball. Aggression was a key word for West Indies fast bowlers, too, although they did not need to say a word to opposition batters to intimidate during their skirmishes.

Richards' county colleague Joel Garner was a prime example of this. A silent giant, standing at 2 metres tall. And someone who frightened me to death.

Prior to him taking up his county contract with Somerset, the Big Bird was a professional at the Central Lancashire League club Littleborough, replacing Sir Garfield Sobers in that guise for the 1976 season, and so would come down to Old Trafford to have a net with the Lancashire first XI, of which I was captain.

It didn't take long for me to make up my mind on a talent like Garner. I wanted Lancashire to sign him for the following season and told the committee so. Unfortunately, however, the club listened to Clive Lloyd, one of our two permitted overseas recruits at that time, who wanted to bring Colin Croft along with him.

The upshot was that Garner was invited to go and take the new ball for Somerset that following summer and as an opening batsman it was my task to go and handle what he threw down at us. I confess he put the fear of God in me every time I faced him for the rest of my career. Some of the best bowlers, they say, are able to add a yard of pace with a click of the fingers. Garner, I felt, added two every single time I was in his sights.

Garner being 6ft 8ins, it was an intimidating proposition if you were stood 20 yards away in anticipation of one of his deliveries. The first thing I saw in his delivery stride was six studs on the sole of his left boot.

'He's going to tread on me,' I cowered.

Or do similar damage to my feet with his famed toe-crushing yorkers. I played against him half a dozen times and on each occasion he slipped a gear. He could have bowled me out with a bath sponge.

There were no words on the field of play. He had the fast bowler's glare down to a tee and so it would be a look but no more. However, an added dimension of his intimidatory hold over me was that, despite his amiable reputation, he was none too friendly towards me off the field. I would not say rude. Just not warm, as he was with others.

Years later, I was to find out why. I was on an England tour of the Caribbean in 2015 in my duties with Sky Sports and Garner was president of the Barbados Cricket Board. Having received an invitation to the president's suite at the Kensington Oval, it placed me in his company.

Previous conversations between us had been a bit stilted but being forced into this environment broke the ice.

'You're the man who never rated me,' he said, in that lovely Bajan drawl.

I was taken aback. He'd been my career nemesis, for goodness' sake.

'You never signed me!'

Barely able to get my words out, I made sure I did so: 'Believe me, *I* wanted to sign you! You've got the wrong Lloyd!'

And with that, a vendetta that had lasted nearly 40 years was broken as he collapsed in a fit of laughter.

I certainly didn't want to be on the wrong side of West Indies' great fast bowlers. Indeed, my policy was to go out of my way *not* to upset them.

Malcolm Marshall was one of the most economical bowlers in the history of the game. I am not talking about economy rates here, rather the physical effort that appeared to go into his bowling. Everything looked so easy for him when he was approaching the crease and from a rhythmical delivery stride the ball would come out of his hand at 90 mph. In his pomp, his bowling was best described as graceful savagery. Aesthetically pleasing with a physical threat.

When I was England coach I was able to get Macko in as a bowler consultant and one of the things that I wanted him to get across to our group of seamers was how to bowl at tail-enders.

'Break their hands,' he said. 'They can't bowl at you then.'

Marshall provided accuracy, pace and great artistry with the ball, particularly later in his career. He was a 100 per center and everyone at Hampshire loved him to bits. Sometimes we play commentators' bingo among our broad-casting gang for a bit of fun and if you listen to Mark Nicholas when he is on air, you lose the number of times he refers to Marshall's greatness.

Marshall took on the baton in Southampton from Andy Roberts, the Antiguan fast bowler, who the other West Indies internationals of that time considered to be the best of the lot of them. But they shared an economy of words on the field.

I once got out first ball to Marshall, caught at slip, during the first innings of a County Championship contest down at the old county ground in Southampton. No shame in that but it left me on a king pair and no one wants one of those. It meant I had to find a response in the second innings.

When someone as consistently good as Marshall keeps running in at you, you have to have a solid game plan and mine was always based around a trigger movement of back and across. On this occasion, I got that far back I could have been stood behind the stumps.

It always felt as if Macko was running straight for you and that his close fielders were suffocating you. Short leg was as close as could be, ready to snaffle any fends off the body.

My tactic for the bouncer on this particular pitch, which was not a quick one, was to stand up and play it defensively. Right back in front of my stumps, I played one in front of my nose, the ball dropping at my feet.

One of Marshall's idiosyncrasies was that he could extend his follow-through via a trademark sideways shimmy down the pitch. It left him stood about 3 metres from me, surveying where my feet had ended up.

'You're going back further at this end than I am at my end,' he said.

To which I retorted: 'That's because you're remarkably fast, sir.'

I hope he didn't mind me calling him 'sir'!

Believe me it was a battle, and there wasn't a single expletive or piece of nastiness. One of the greats was trying to get me out and in turn I was trying to defy him. Truly, those that belonged to the great West Indies outfit never said a word.

Yet the modern trend globally has been to abuse opponents. I noted with interest when Kevin Pietersen was on commentary for England's tour of South Africa in 2019–20 and, in response to some expletives from Jos Buttler to Vernon Philander, said: 'This is Test cricket. This is how it should be. This is what it's all about.'

Michael Holding interjected that he just didn't agree with it. 'I have a bowl, you have a bat, let's play cricket,' he said.

It was an old school versus new kid debate, I guess, based on whatever you are brought up with. Two blokes from different generations and backgrounds. But is it right to have foul language on the field? In 19 years I cannot recall anybody abusing me. Don't get me wrong, I liked a chat. Just not cheap talk.

From the mid-1960s, in a bid to drum up interest in the English game and attract bigger crowds, counties had voted to allow one overseas player per team if they adhered to a two-year residency criterion. Namely making their adopted county their home. Pakistan's Mushtaq Mohammad and Basil D'Oliveira, who would go on to play for England after leaving apartheid South Africa, were among the first influx.

By 1968, a second imported player could be recruited immediately with three caveats: anyone who signed would not be eligible to join a rival county for three years; a county could not replace that player for three years regardless of whether they left; and the county could have a maximum of two overseas players.

In 2019 when the inaugural Hundred draft took place, Afghanistan's Rashid Khan was the hot pick of the global scene and went as the number one choice to Trent Rockets. Just over half a century earlier, the altering of the regulations led to multiple suitors for Sir Garry Sobers. Nottingham was the destination for him, too, the best bid on the table accompanied by the club captaincy.

Weeks later, while England were on a Test tour of West Indies, Sobers made a bold prediction of the team he inherited, suggesting to tour manager Les Ames's wife, Bunty, that despite perennial bottom-four finishes for a decade, the following year would see them in the top four. A wager of six bottles of champagne was made between the pair and the corks were popping upon the conclusion of *that* match at Swansea when Sobers struck six sixes in an over from Malcolm Nash in a decisive win.

Of all the all-rounders, when asked which of them was the best I came up against, I would always say Sobers. Why?

Because he was such an influential cricketer when I was kid coming through the ranks. Someone who could bat, bowl all variations of left arm with the ball, and field. Because of his attributes, he could adapt to any situation throughout the course of a game and have an influence.

West Indians were the most prevalent among the influx – not surprisingly, as they were the world's dominant team, and also considering England was the one destination where cricketers were truly full-time professionals pre-Kerry Packer's involvement in Australia. But there were a clutch of Pakistan cricketers who made counties their homes over the next dozen years.

I remember Imran Khan when he played for Oxford University as a filthy in-swing bowler. I should add a filthy, *slow* in-swing bowler because only towards the end of his first county stint with Worcestershire did he start to run in and bowl like we all now remember him.

County cricket definitely provided him with the opportunity to get fit and it wasn't long into his time as an overseas player that you could see he was developing into a great cricketer. While a student at Oxford he just wasn't going anywhere, but once into the professional ranks you could see him getting quicker and quicker year on year to the point at Sussex where he and Garth Le Roux steamed in from either end in a terrifying new-ball attack.

He was such a gentle pace as a bowler in his youth that the wicketkeeper would stand up on occasion. Wide of the crease with a fall-away action, he was about 10–15 mph slower than what he ended up. I guess he worked out for himself that he would be so much more effective if he ran in aggressively. He got closer to the stumps and followed through and suddenly: BOOM.

From a national team perspective, Imran became the leader of Pakistan, just as he is in a political sense now, and everyone followed him. He was a born leader and Wasim Akram, someone I know well from our time at Lancashire together, revered him. Imran was great for Pakistan cricket because he would look after the young players like Wasim coming through, promoting their abilities and therefore suitability to be picked in the team. It didn't matter how many matches they hadn't played – all he cared about was whether they were the best available options to play in the next match.

It was a policy that served Pakistan well, particularly during the 1992 World Cup when young players like Wasim, Inzaman-ul-Haq and Aaqib Javed emerged. If Imran, as captain, said you were in, you were in. They were real raw talents, but he had an eye for a cricketer.

Away from the field he was an absolute playboy. Ladies used to swoon over him. He'd have a string of beauties on his arm and be in all the big nightclubs in London during the 1970s. Later, he got to do what he really set out to and that was serving in politics. He has used the vehicle of cricket to communicate with his people and I was intrigued by his Sky Sports interview with Michael Atherton in which he explained his vision for Pakistan and the world and the fact he had kept achieving in life by constantly challenging himself. I've always liked the way he has chaptered his life. The end game is that he has arrived at where he wanted to be. What a job that is to have on the CV.

Of course, that means he has to stand up to Donald Trump and all the other world leaders, but he has never shirked a challenge and it is clear that his life has been devoted to the betterment of Pakistan. It is some country and it is sad that it has had so many problems. It used to be a fabulous place to tour. I have such fond memories of touring Pakistan when I was coach and Adam Hollioake was captain: down in the markets in Lahore after practice one day, playing cricket in the streets with young children, riding elephants and joining locals at the gigantic Badshahi Mosque.

Imran had that fierce rivalry with Ian Botham and it was sad that it ended up with a £500,000 libel case in the High Court. They were two great warriors and it shouldn't have got to that stage. There was great rivalry between several all-rounders at that time. And Imran could bat, too. Remember, he sent himself in at a number three in the 1992 World Cup final and it proved an inspired decision.

During their rivalry Imran and Beefy were about the same pace. Until Botham's back went, he was very slippery. Imran's big thing was reverse swing. He could get the ball booming into the batsman from that wide angle on the crease – a hand-me-down gift from Sarfraz Nawaz and one passed onto Aaqib, Wasim and Waqar.

It was looked down upon for quite some time with so much innuendo over its legitimacy, but what a great skill it was and how ahead of their time they were in comparison to other countries. These days, no fast bowler in the world is complete without an ability to get a deteriorated ball to duck this way and that.

Javed Miandad made a career of upsetting people. One of the most famous photographs in cricket history depicts the Pakistan batsman with his bat raised, poised to land a blow on legendary Australian bowler Dennis Lillee in a Test match in Perth in 1981. That he didn't was partly due to the quick thinking of the diminutive umpire Tony Crafter trying to keep the peace between them.

Miandad's retaliation came after he was kicked up the bum by the bowler after the pair collided in mid-pitch. Tensions cooled but Lillee still received a two-match ban and hefty fine for provocation.

Usually it's the bowlers that start things off with a word or two. Not when Javed was playing, though. He would be the antagonist, having a chip at anybody if he felt it would help gain the upper hand, and he would deliberately stand out of his ground to try to get the fielders to have a shy. He knew how overthrows not only frustrated opponents but often got them arguing among themselves. He was constantly trying to engage the opposition – and destabilise them.

There was a classic example of this when Glamorgan hosted Lancashire at Cardiff just a few months before that fracas with Lillee on the other side of the world.

It was the fourth innings of the match and Jack Simmons, who bowled quick off-spin and was known as Flat Jack because of its trajectory, was wheeling away in the Lancashire quest for victory. As the side's front-line spinner, the final day of Championship matches in which we batted first were the ones in which our substantial Simmons would come into his own.

It was the last ball of the over and Javed had come out of his crease and patted the ball just beyond where silly point might have been, pressing onto his tiptoes and feigning to run despite the lack of any distance on the stroke.

'Come, Fat Jack,' Javed goaded, inviting his opponent to pick up the ball, just a couple of yards away.

Of course, there had been nothing lost in translation for the Pakistani, who knew full well that Jack – an ample chap who would delight in making sure all three courses were taken at lunch before returning to the field for an afternoon session – would be fuming at being called fat rather than flat.

As Javed inched forward, so did Jack, to the point where the chance of a run-out became too tempting to ignore. Bounding into no man's land, he seized upon the ball and flung it at the stumps. The nimble-footed batsman turned to make his ground and watched with glee as the ball passed its intended target and fizzed across the outfield.

Peter Lee had been positioned at deep backward square leg but, with it being the last ball of the over, had vacated the area in anticipation of bowling from the other end, and was therefore powerless to intercept. The four overthrows simply enraged Simmons further. In fact, he was left apoplectic, punching his cap and muttering to himself. I worried he was going to explode.

'Don't let him get to you. He's trying to rile you, Jack,' David Hughes told him.

'You're too late. He already has bloody riled me!' came the reply.

As the chief wind-up merchant of his generation, Javed just had that effect on people. On this occasion, Jack had the last laugh, taking the catch that dismissed him for 72 in a 66-run victory.

Rarely was Javed deterred from picking a squabble, the intention always being to put opponents off their game. Although he was known to have backed down while he was playing as a professional in the Northern League. On one occasion, he had a pop at Ken Snellgrove, who spent several years on the playing staff at Old Trafford. Snelly, a Scouser, had got fed up even with some of Javed's mild antagonism on this particular occasion and wandered over to him from his fielding position at point and warned: 'Say another word and I'll have you shot!' Reports have it that the sound level on the field of play after that point were the equivalent of the mute button being pressed.

But what I admired about Javed was his impassioned defence of Pakistan – his patriotism would not allow his country's honour to be questioned – and his individual brilliance. Yes, he was a fighter when it came to battles on the field but his gifts as a batsman were not those normally associated with a battler. He was not a grafter, the kind of batter that dug in and based his innings on defence, but a real touch player.

I always thought he was a similar character to Sri Lanka's World Cup-winning captain Arjuna Ranatunga in the way that he could get under opponents' skins and force bowlers to lose concentration. It would contribute to the opposition losing their dominance and more often than not losing the game. Team plans that had been in place before the innings had started would be cast aside and forgotten about and they would start taking him on as an individual. That's not what they were out there to do.

And he had the skills to expose undisciplined bowling through his great hands and footwork, as good as I've seen throughout my years in the game. He had such nimble movement down the pitch, allowing him to get to the ball on the full or half-volley and strike it into the gaps he was targeting. He was a consistent scorer of runs and the thing I used to think about him was that he didn't go through bad times, through dips in form; he always seemed to be successful.

People might question how he was against the fastest bowling. He was absolutely fine. He'd take anybody on. Extreme pace, exaggerated seam or spin. He was extremely difficult to get out. Especially in Pakistan – where it was an urban myth that the home umpires did not give him out lbw. The truth was that he was not dismissed leg before wicket on home soil between his Test debut in 1976 and a match versus Sri Lanka in October 1985. Still, nine years is a fair period of immunity.

And so, as a result, if he found himself upon a particularly dodgy pitch he would get in front of the stumps knowing that he was seldom going to be dismissed lbw. Neutral umpires for Test matches came as a result of such reputations, with touring teams increasingly distrusting officials they considered 'homers'.

It was Javed's Pakistan team of 1987–88 that featured in

a diplomatic incident with England in Faisalabad, although the home captain was not involved directly. Questionable decisions from the first Test had already caused irritation in the touring camp but in the second, courtesy of a competitive score of 292 on a sporting pitch, England were in the ascendancy with Pakistan 106 for five at the end of day two.

Eddie Hemmings was bowling his off-spin to Salim Malik and, keen to get an extra over in before stumps to pressure the debutant Aamer Malik, Mike Gatting, England's captain and short leg, summoned David Capel in from the square-leg boundary to save a single, telling the batsman of his action.

But with Hemmings about to start his run-up, Gatting realised Capel had come too far and gestured from behind his back for him to stop. Shakoor Rana, the square-leg umpire, decided to intervene, halting play and accusing Gatting of sharp practice.

'You are waving your hand. That's cheating,' Shakoor said, when Gatting questioned his intervention.

Gatt said he had not been waving, merely telling the fielder to come no closer, that he had informed the batsman the fielder was moving and it was the duty of the non-striker to keep his partner up to speed, not the square-leg umpire.

Told to return whence he came, Shakoor did just that but could not suppress the use of the *ch* word and the *c* word as he did so. Cue the famous finger-wagging and an official apology from Gatt. As I say, Javed loved to see the other team rattled and this would have been no different.

The relationship between the Pakistan and England

cricket teams was fraught throughout that decade but once in retirement Javed held no grudges. On one tour, while we were out commentating on the series, he invited us round to his house, which was a converted government building. I have never seen a house as big – it was like the town hall. Absolutely enormous.

Geoffrey Boycott was with us and as one who habitually refused to stand on ceremony, asked, 'Now Javed, you've invited us over, when can we have some food?' That's Geoffrey and his forthright ways for you!

Another lovely player from Pakistan was Sadiq Mohammad – a superb batsman but a very reluctant fielder. He just didn't seem to like it. I came to that conclusion because he didn't seem to do much of it.

If he made a hundred in the first innings of a one-day match, as he did with 122 off us in the 1975 Gillette Cup semi-final in Manchester, you knew damn well that he wouldn't be coming back out for the second. He would develop a limp as he trudged off the field, struggle to negotiate the steps back up to the dressing room and then settle in and make himself comfortable inside while Gloucestershire sent on a lad called Jim Foat.

Now Foat wouldn't get into their team very often but was a real gun fielder, a bit like Gary Pratt, the man who despite playing on the county circuit for a decade is known exclusively for running out Ricky Ponting in an Ashes Test match at Trent Bridge. Like a gazelle running around the field and one of the best there was when it came to fielding.

With Sadiq and Zaheer Abbas in the top six, and Mike

Procter spearheading the bowling attack, Gloucestershire were a great side. They were a great team to play against, one of the best of that era, and were always pushing us for one-day trophies through the 1970s. All players want to play against the best teams and we had some cracking cup matches over the years. For the record, Sadiq claimed the man of the match award and Foat two catches, but we were the ones that progressed to Lord's, and a final meeting with Middlesex, via a three-wicket-victory margin.

There were some really prolific run-getters who came here to earn a living during that period of multiple overseas players per team. Among them, Glenn Turner, an odd chap but a thoroughbred player who owed his worldwide success to his enrolment in county cricket's finishing school. His ambitions as a batter were modest when he arrived but it helped him develop every shot in the book and the versatility to adapt to contrasting challenges.

One particular innings for Worcestershire stands out for me, and you will soon see why. It came at Swansea during the 1977 season when, during a match against Glamorgan, he ended the first day unbeaten on 39 in a visitors' total of 44 for two.

In between the close and the resumption next morning, Turner spent the evening with Bob Blair, the ex-New Zealand international, and drink was taken. Lots of it. In the form of gin and tonics. It meant Turner had to resume his innings with a hangover.

Jim Cumbes, the nightwatchman, kept him company for the majority of the first hour but his dismissal sparked a collapse of six wickets for 15 runs to leave Worcestershire 93 for eight.

Faced with what he believed was a good pitch, Turner continued with his one-man batting salvo, helping his team avoid the follow-on by carrying his bat for 141. Worcestershire's total was just 169, making the Kiwi's contribution the highest proportion of a completed innings in first-class cricket at 83.4 per cent.

It reminded me of a similar episode in my own career. My late cousin, Jack Aspin, was an Anonymous chap, being both an alcoholic and a gambler.

There can have been no meetings on one particular evening, however – the second of a three-day match versus Gloucestershire in 1973 – as Jack and I were chewing the fat over a few drinks until five o'clock in the morning in the local Conservative Club, at which time the secretary of said club had the temerity to throw us out (Jack falling down the stairs in the process).

After a couple of hours' shut-eye, I was then required to return to Old Trafford where a bowling attack, led by the brilliant Mike Procter, was intent on pushing for the victory their strong overnight position merited.

The Lancashire team, of which I was captain, trailed by 250 runs on first innings and had erased 47 from it for the loss of one wicket prior to the third and final day in Manchester. Resuming on 36, with nightwatchman Jack Simmons for company, I finished up with 195, hitting the ball to all parts and unleashing an array of shots not normally associated with my batting. It was one of the best innings I ever played, helping to secure a draw with some comfort. And I can't remember it!

Equally, I have never known whether to be grateful to David Baron, the Conservative Club secretary in question, for intervening as he did or whether I might have scored even more on no kip at all.

David, who attended those Alcoholics Anonymous meetings with Jack, was my next-door neighbour in Accrington at the time. Daily he would take the family dog, a standard poodle, for a long walk to give it some exercise.

Until one day when he felt rather unwell and the task was passed to Mrs Baron, whose elocution was rather incongruous with a Lancashire mill town. All was going well on said walk apparently until the dog got excitable, broke from her grasp and, with the lead trailing behind, bolted into the Alma Inn.

Upon entering, and finding the canine up on a stool at the bar, she addresses the landlord in Hyacinth Bucket tones.

'Ever so sorry, I don't know what came over him,' she says. 'I will get him down immediately.'

'Oh, don't worry, it's the usual spot. He's in here every lunchtime.'

Rumbled. I never was, mind. Although I am not sure there could have been too many complaints from any of the committee at Old Trafford. On reflection, perhaps I should have tested the merits of a skinful before every innings.

To be fair to Turner, whose exquisite timing of the ball put him among the best in that regard that the game has ever seen, he had plenty of big knocks to recall as only the second non-Englishman to hit 100 first-class hundreds after

Sir Donald Bradman. But emulating the routines of Tom Graveney, the club's seasoned professional when he joined the New Road staff, may have contributed to his recall of others' contributions being a tad hazier. Graveney had a reputation for being last in the bar at night, first at nets in the morning.

Let me fill in the background on this one. It was a tour of New Zealand and Glenn, a former national coach and selector for the Kiwis, walked into the media centre, shook hands with Michael Atherton and Jonathan Agnew, and they chatted for a while.

He then asked Aggers: 'Would you like to come round and have dinner?'

Agnew replied: 'That would be lovely, Glenn. Thanks very much.'

So, over the course of the evening, they are reminiscing about old times. Mainly county cricket, as Turner was a stalwart. He would be saying things like 'And do you remember this match when I got x amount of runs . . . and such and such a body did this . . . and then that happened . . .'

And Aggers, nonplussed, would reply: 'No, no, I don't remember that, actually.'

'What about when we did this . . . and when Whozit played the innings of his life . . . and what about that spell . . .'

'No, I don't think that was me. I wasn't involved in that match. I'm sure I wasn't.'

By now Agnew has plucked up enough courage to challenge his host for the evening with: 'You don't actually know who I am, do you?'

To which Turner had to confess: 'No.'

That snippet summed up Glenn Turner for me. A wonderful player but absent-minded. As they say, it certainly takes all sorts.

CHAPTER 8

The Officials

When it comes to those men in the middle, the arbiters of fair play without whom there would be no game, there has been no more famous figure than Harold 'Dickie' Bird.

Believe me, from the experience of standing for three seasons as a first-class umpire between 1985 and 1987, it is a thankless task trying to please everyone. Your decisions can displease one team or the other, and sometimes both in quick succession, and those watching the game always seem to have an opinion on your performance.

So how do you keep everyone happy? One thing that Dickie had was the respect of the players. He had played the game, lived the game and loved the game. A nervous so-and-so as a young player, he used that positively when he joined the men in white coats, gaining a reputation for being fully prepared from the word go. This undoubtedly had something to do with the fact that his fretting about turning up late for his second first-team assignment at The Oval caused him to report to said ground at 6 a.m. It's a fair effort to beat a groundsman to work.

Dickie *was* cricket, and his personality, undeniably eccentric, was also infectious.

He also learnt to live with the pressures of officiating at the highest level with a smile on his face. Several comedic moments come to mind when you think back over his career. Here was a man who umpired in multiple World Cup finals. Yet the images of him people might recall most fondly would involve his histrionics when there was no play.

Due to the wet weather that had plagued the build-up, the start of the England v West Indies Test match at Headingley in 1988 had been delayed. There had been a torrential downpour on the previous evening and chances of play getting underway on time looked bleak.

Bleak enough, in fact, for the water hogs that usually wallowed at Trent Bridge, Old Trafford and Edgbaston to be transported across the country's motorway network to Leeds. With these hired machines at their disposal, the ground staff, led by Keith Boyce, did a miraculous job in removing the excess water off the playing area and as a result the game started just an hour late.

Not that it lasted very long, though. Just four deliveries to be exact before what initially seemed to be an unexplained break in play.

Curtly Ambrose was bowling to Graham Gooch but instead of this fast-bowling beanpole surging past a hunched Dickie for a fifth time, he made it to the halfway mark of his approach and stood motionless.

'Mr Dickie, we got problems here, man,' Curtly yells.

Those problems were evident when Dickie turned and joined the West Indies great in about 10 Curtly strides, and therefore two dozen Dickie steps, away from his position at the non-striker's end.

Ambrose was paddling about in puddles that had begun seeping through the turf, so Dickie shouted across to his colleague David Shepherd at square leg.

'We've got a problem, Shep. There's water oozing up.'

'Throw some sawdust down,' was Shep's first proposed solution.

Only when Shep trundled over and saw the water rising up and soaking the boots did the extent of the problem become clear to him.

'We've got to take them off,' he says.

'What, and paddle about in bare feet?'

'Not the boots, you fool.'

As the players left the field, Dickie, who seemed to be cursed whenever he went back to officiate at Headingley, knew he was going take some stick.

'They'll lynch me,' he told his partner.

And the Yorkshire crowd were not in a mood to disappoint him, someone shouting as he made his way to the old pavilion: 'You're here again, Bird. Every time you come to Headingley, you're bringing 'em off. What is it this time? What's the problem now?'

Bird could be heard on television, as the cameras panned to follow his exit from the field, saying: 'I can't help it, can I? There's a burst pipe and water's coming up. Not my fault, that. You don't need an umpire out there, you need a plumber.'

Neither was he immune from criticism when he trekked over the Pennines. Take the 1995 Test match against the Windies when sun – of all things – stopped play. The reflections off greenhouses outside the ground, and hospitality box windows within it, were blinding the tourists' batsman. Off on one, striding over the advertising boards, to roars and jeers.

He was also the target for the high jinks of players. Allan Lamb was a serial offender in this regard and once managed to talk Dickie into looking after his mobile phone during the 1983 Test match between England and New Zealand at Trent Bridge.

Lamb had taken it to the crease with him when it was his turn to bat and persuaded Dickie, a nervous character at the best of times, to keep it safe. And 'answer it, if it rings'.

The persuasion worked and after a fairly uneventful first 10 minutes to Lamb's innings, said phone began to ring. Clearly having forgotten what he was concealing in his top pocket, Dickie looked about him not realising where the noise was coming from. When the penny dropped, he shouted across to Lamb.

'Answer it, then,' came the reply.

Surreptitiously, he attempted to do so. No mean feat when there is a full house and live television coverage.

'Hello, this is Dickie Bird, speaking on Allan Lamb's phone,' he whispered. 'Who's that?'

'This is Ian Botham ringing from the dressing

room – would you please tell that fella Lamb to start playing a few shots or get out!'

Lamb was forever playing tricks on officialdom and was one for putting smoke bombs under umpires' doors for a laugh. More of that later.

When it came to judging his decisions, Dickie was arguably afflicted by the nervous disposition that used to see him chew his batting gloves as a batsman with Yorkshire and Leicestershire. He would agonise over his response to appeals and always stuck to his rule of thumb: if in doubt, give it not out.

Until technology became so prevalent in the decision-making process at international level, umpires used to be on their own, and had only a few seconds to make up their minds. How you came to that decision was important. Some deliberated and took what seemed to be an eternity to put their fingers up. Others had a much more shotgun approach.

But as I say, Dickie was a not-outer throughout his career. To stand at the other end to him was an event and I stood with him in a pre-season fixture involving Oxford University at The Parks in 1986 when he told me: 'Now you see these here lads, these students, they are just playing cricket for a bit of fun and they haven't come to be given out lbw.'

And so if you were with him in a university match, you could not give leg befores, even nailed-on ones. To be fair, though, Dickie didn't give anybody out lbw. Or only in leap years. They were certainly not a regular occurrence. You get my drift.

During my playing days, on the rare occasion he gave me

lbw, you could see it ate him up and he would apologise after the game. 'I really didn't want to give you, you know. I mean, I couldn't stop. I mean, it were absolutely plumb one. I'm really sorry that I had to give you. Forgive me.'

Of course, you already had – because it was Dickie. You knew where you stood with him.

Funnily enough, though, the umpire with a reputation for being the players' friend was Ray Julian, despite being the opposite of Dickie. When I say he was the players' friend, I should qualify that by saying that he was the friend of a particular sub-set of players. All the bowlers wanted to bowl at his end because they knew their chances of success would be improved. A nightmare for batters, bowlers loved him. But he was consistent because he didn't favour either team. What kind of a character was he, then? Unbelievably friendly. He just had a regular twitch that resulted in his right index finger being raised.

Ray, a former wicketkeeper with Leicestershire, used to keep a little black book of his lbws, and he was hell-bent every season on getting 100 for a first-class season, taking the logging process seriously enough to write the dismissals down in three sections:

Definitely

Marginal

Probably missing

Sounds like an Oasis comeback album, doesn't it?

Underneath each heading he would add ticks for every applicable dismissal.

I was on duty at Trent Bridge as junior umpire to Mr Julian

in the era of Richard Hadlee and Clive Rice. And he said: 'Which end would you like to stand at today, Mr Lloyd?'

'Well, you're the senior umpire, Mr Julian, you can choose,' I responded, showing him the respect our respective ranks merited.

'Well, I'll stand at Mr Hadlee's end because I can feel a five-for coming on here,' he declared. 'All lbw!'

On another occasion in July 1987 at St Helen's, Swansea, a lovely ground next to the sea with about 80 steps leading from the changing rooms down to the boundary edge, Glamorgan were playing Northamptonshire, myself and Julian were standing and a second early wicket falls.

Having ground their way to 305 all out, Glamorgan had reduced the visitors to five for two before lunch on day two, and the ball is doing enough to keep both Ray and I on our toes.

He shouted across: 'Have you seen who is coming in now?' I looked and who was coming down those 80 steps? I recognised the squat figure of an established England batsman.

So I say: 'It's A. J. Lamb.'

'You're absolutely right there,' he said. 'I bet I get him before you do!'

Anyway, he had been in for about 10 minutes or so when Steve Barwick rapped him on the pads, there was a big appeal, and Julian gives him out for two.

'There you are, Mr Lloyd, what did I tell you?'

As a result, Northants were reduced to 23 for three and were four down soon afterwards when we came off the field for lunch.

Unbeknownst to us, Lamb, a larger-than-life character whose preferred form of retribution was of the mischievous rather than menacing variety, had managed to commandeer the pavilion keys off the dressing-room attendant, Eddie, during the 40-minute interval and locked us in the umpires' room. Not only did he lock the door, he slipped under the bottom of the door a copy of the *Daily Telegraph*. Alight.

So we're putting a fire out for the start, then the bell goes and we can't get out. The players restarted the game with no umpires, although nobody on the ground seemed to notice. The players were appealing. After an over, Lamb let us out and only when two blokes in white jackets came on down the steps was it clocked.

Games were generally played in a relaxed atmosphere. On this occasion, arguably too relaxed, and it was to cost Glamorgan dear. Despite taking a 96-run lead on first innings, they had capitulated to 50 for seven by the close, were dismissed for 77, and lost by eight wickets with Lamb at the crease for the winning runs.

Raymond had a very colourful love life. He has settled down now in Somerset with the lovely Megan, but he used to be married to a lass called Ruth, and they travelled around in a caravan.

That week in South Wales we had a double booking. Northants' visit on the first, second and third of the month was immediately followed by another three-day game against Gloucestershire on the fourth, fifth and sixth.

Umpiring for six days on the trot is demanding on one's concentration levels. The days were long – although the 110 overs required in six and a half hours was a cut from the 117 that were required to be bowled in Championship matches up until 1984 – and so you didn't want to have to travel too far from the ground to your digs.

That made Ray's travelling arrangements ideal. He had moored his caravan on the rugby pitch, which is right next to the cricket complex, right next to one of the sets of goalposts.

We were almost at the end of the match, the last day of three. It was a dusty pitch, it was stinking hot and Gloucestershire had lots of men around the bat as David Graveney and Jeremy Lloyds bowled in tandem, and seemed to be appealing every other delivery. It was a real dig-in for the home batsmen and after concentrating very hard, you just wanted to get off for tea. For a cuppa, a shower and a towel-down.

But after five full days on a makeshift campsite, there was another problem to contend with on day six, and both sets of teams were about to discover what it was as Ruth bounded onto the pitch from the adjacent one as we were wandering off.

'Raymond,' she said. 'We've run out of milk!'

As you contemplate a cuppa, I give you food for thought that the umpire was guaranteed tremendous respect from all the players in previous eras regardless of whether they were notorious not-outers like Syd Buller or a shooter-from-the-hip like Eddie Phillipson. You would certainly accept decisions more stoically than in subsequent ones. Some of that has to do with societal changes, I am sure.

When I first started playing in the 1960s, we were a lot less inclined to challenge authority and therefore the umpires ruled the roost. Men like Charlie Elliott and Buller. We called them Mr Elliott and Mr Buller. Later on, as you played more, you called them Charlie and Syd. But you had to earn their respect by meeting the expected level of etiquette. For example, if you wanted a team-collected drink, they could just say no, and if that is what they said you didn't get one.

And if a 12th man came on unscheduled or unannounced, the first thing the umpire would say is: 'What do you want?' If the officials weren't satisfied that it was a legitimate interruption, or they were feeling that way inclined, he on 'twelfths' would have to go off.

And you would have to grin and bear some of their filthy personal habits. No, it wasn't quite the Victorian era of umpires smoking pipes. This was something else filling the nostrils. You see, Bill Alley and Cec Pepper both suffered from undue flatulence. Unbelievable.

You could be bowling and they would let one rip in your run-up. It can put a man off his game, you know. Or they would stand at square leg, lift their legs and you would hear the parp from wherever you were positioned on the field.

Yet this rather anti-social habit belied their otherwise sociable demeanours. Neither ever stopped talking. They'd be talking to the non-striking batter, talking to the bowler, talking to the mid-off fielder, to anybody within earshot.

But the daddy of them all was Arthur Jepson, who kept goal for Port Vale and Stoke City among others in winters and bowled seam up in summers. He had two very distinctive features did Arthur. One was his hair that he used to have plastered down with either Silvikrin or Brylcreem. The other was his voice, which was like a foghorn. To the extent that he would be at square leg holding a conversation, thinking he was whispering, and you could hear him in the stand.

And he didn't mind an opinion, either. As a young lad, I once came on to bowl my left-arm spin at his end. I had just given him my cap when he said: 'I hope you don't mind me mentioning this but you're the worst bowler I've ever seen.'

How about that for an ice-breaker? I bet he'd have been a whizz at speed dating.

'Fred Price were bad. But you're worse than him,' he continued.

To put this into context, dear reader, it must be disclosed that Price was a renowned cricketer of 400 first-class appearances, including one in a Test match for England in the 1938 Ashes. But he was a stumper and therefore did not bowl a single ball in 20 years. So I was being compared to a bowler who would only have been witnessed lobbing them up in the nets.

As I say, he was not shy of a strong opinion. Once, he was at square leg and Neal Radford, who was a bloody good cricketer and someone who blossomed after he left Lancashire and went to Worcestershire, was bowling for us. Radford was known for his shuffling run-up and short fuse.

'Can this bloke bat?' Arthur whispered. Of course, everybody in the same postcode could hear him.

'Yeah,' I told him. 'He's a decent lower-order player.'

'Well, that's good, cos he can't f***ing bowl, can he? He looks like he needs a shit.'

He came out with some classic one-liners, did Arthur.

None more famous than during that 1971 Gillette Cup semi-final match against Gloucestershire when Jack Bond, our captain at Lancashire, appealed against the light.

'I can see the moon up there. How much further do you want to see?' Arthur said to him. As it turned out, Jack and David Hughes proved good enough to deal with a ball being hurled down at them from 22 yards and victory was secured after 9 p.m.

Jepson, nicknamed Dinky, was such a great man of our game that he could literally say anything and nobody would care. He used to stop at Jack Simmons's house when he was doing Old Trafford matches. He was a real personality of the era.

And that is how the game has changed. They were just great company, umpires. I'm not saying it was a laugh a minute, but it was certainly a laugh having them around.

So why have those relationships changed? Well, the stakes have been raised too high for starters. We used to be on the circuit together, travelling round, all trying to do our best. But there was an acceptance that we would all make mistakes. The game of cricket was played in a more Corinthian spirit. Prize money was only introduced in 1973, and a minimum wage of £4,000 for capped players agreed six years later. People were involved in county cricket because they loved being a part of it all. These days it is a highly paid career choice.

The reaction to the picking of the seam by a bowler 50 years ago to what it would be now represents two ends of the spectrum. Tampering had always been a big thing for bowlers, although they wouldn't have got away with doing it every week.

At Lancashire, we had Peter Lee, who allegedly could have a little nibble and one day his performance raised suspicion with another of the revered officials of the time in Bill Alley. Bill asked to look at the ball and as someone who allegedly could have a pick of the seam when he was playing, looked at it, threw it back and said: 'You've made a good job of that, Leapy. If you don't get several wickets, I'll report you.'

That's just how things were, and players were very affectionate towards the umpires because of it. They had been there and done it, and knew all the tricks of the trade.

It was a different era. Why was it different? Because of the lack of scrutiny via technology. Back then, you would have very few cameras at televised matches, so even for Test matches and one-day internationals the umpire remained king.

Now, with the Decision Review System (DRS), it is all about challenging the authority of the decision. 'The umpire has made a mistake,' is a common theme in cricket chat. Well, mistakes are so much easier to notice when 30-plus cameras are being used to pick up every minute detail and people are on the case to spot them.

Both the relationship and the balance of power have changed between umpires and players. It's now a well-paid job to be an international umpire but they've worked hard to have a demeanour which defuses a situation. Study closely and you will recognise that the ICC's elite umpires are all very passive, exuding calm even when players are going apoplectic. They just turn the other way.

Today's best umpires in Aleem Dar, Kumar Dharmasena, Marais Erasmus and Chris Gaffaney – the guys who are awarded the highest-profile assignments – know that their decisions will be challenged regularly by the players through the application of the DRS and, as an extension of that, they will also be challenged by commentators. I hope I have a reputation for leniency on air in this regard, as an ex-official myself.

While some jump in with: 'He's made a mistake.' My response to that would be: 'Of course he's made a mistake. He's human. You ever done it?'

DRS can correct mistakes if they are made and statistics will highlight that decision-making has improved out of sight. I hope players respect the fact that technology also shows that more than 95 per cent of calls made by umpires are right first time.

Remember, some players wouldn't tour back in the day because the umpiring was so biased. They viewed it as a pointless journey. New Zealand was notorious at one stage. Look no further than the actions of Michael Holding, one of the most placid cricketers you could ever meet, kicking the stumps out of the ground in Dunedin in 1980.

The Kiwi officials were notorious for favouring the home side and in this instance John Hastie flicked the switch of someone who never lost his rag, ever, when he failed to acknowledge the fact that John Parker had nicked behind. Holding volleying the stumps from their holes in the ground is one of world cricket's most striking images.

There were a few issues in India and Pakistan, too, and

players from the latter tried to get some of the English officials changed during tours here in the 1980s. The need for neutral empires was obvious by that stage, and it has improved the global standard so much.

Occasionally, now, we see teams acting too aggressively towards officialdom and 1 know from my experience of international cricket that some teams have whiteboards in dressing rooms and on some of those whiteboards you'll see it written: challenge the umpire. Coaches will look at who is standing in a match and, if they think he's vulnerable or can be influenced by certain behaviours, they will ask their players to put him under extra pressure as doing so might nudge the individual the fielding side's way.

In an age in which technology ultimately dictates decisions, you might argue that applying such pressure is futile. However, it can still be influential. Consider the application of umpire's call within the DRS protocol. If you can sway the umpire to put his finger up, then it increases the chances of claiming the wicket you seek.

Officials are instructed not to be combative in policing on the field but to work with the players to calm any flashpoint down. Occasionally, though, players need to be reminded of their responsibilities on the field and someone who retired in 2019 in Ian 'Gunner' Gould, a man who cared deeply about the game and its morals, had a fabulously simple way of dealing with individuals who were causing trouble on the field.

Gunner would move from his standing position to get near to the stump microphone when addressing the perpetrator. At which point, he would shout down the pitch to the individual concerned, and made sure he used their name in the address when he said: 'I hoped you were a better person than that.'

That's a great line. All you need to say. It should cut out any nonsense because players don't want to be known to be misbehaving.

In the past, when Syd Buller and Charlie Elliott were in charge, officialdom ruled. Give me the old school any day. In fact, I would like to see things go back to that style. Even in a county game now, the director of cricket or the head coach has every right to go into the umpires' room and ask about a decision. What are you supposed to answer, if asked: why did you give that? I would think it is pretty self-explanatory.

I'm not sure anyone would have challenged another bloke I umpired with – Alan Whitehead. The players were frightened to death of him. With good cause. He could handle himself. You didn't mess with Whitehead.

He liked to go for a lap or two before play to keep fit and when I umpired with him at The Parks for one of Oxford University's early season fixtures, he went off into the environs to extend his morning run. A dog, off its lead, ran after him and bit him. So he walked straight up to the owner, a total stranger, and slotted him one.

This no-nonsense reputation made him a good partner to stand with in matches because you were guaranteed there would be no shit from the players. He'd get straight into them. There was no question about who was dictating to whom. Who was in charge. Any sense of disrespect and he would frighten the life out of them with a simple line: who do you think you're talking to?

When one famously did challenge his authority, during an Ashes Test match at Trent Bridge in 1985, the episode ended with Ian Botham being warned about his future conduct by the Test and County Cricket Board.

Having had a leg-before appeal against Greg Ritchie turned down by Whitehead, Botham was left fuming when a bouncer was caught in the deep only for his fellow man of Somerset to call a no-ball. Further Beefy explosions followed when he was warned about sustained short-pitched bowling and then running on the pitch.

Some would argue that Alan, who his contemporaries reckoned should have been appointed for more Test matches than he received, had a novel way of keeping control on the field. Some would have said it wasn't necessarily an umpire's job to rule with fear and that he was too officious with the way he went about his work.

But he wasn't there to be a friend. He was there to make sure the game was played fairly, and in the right spirit, and he never let anything get out of hand. If it did, as in that Botham incident, he would nip it in the bud straight away or send it higher to be dealt with. The message was clear: 'Just get on with the game.' A little bit later, another English umpire to stand in internationals, Peter Willey, developed a similar reputation.

When I first started, it was the ex-Gloucestershire wicket-keeper Barrie Meyer, by then a well-respected international umpire, who provided me with good advice.

Barrie would talk about the 'business end' for umpires. It wouldn't work these days with all the television cameras because each ball is under such scrutiny. But he would say 'Don't worry too much about this line here, because that's where the business happens, up there,' pointing towards the batsman.

His argument was – and this is something I try to explain on TV regularly – that because of where the umpire generally has to stand, the front foot of any bowler, particularly the quick bowlers, tends to be obscured by his own body. Hence, the umpire can't see that front foot and whether or not any of it is behind the line.

So what we tended to do was get the bowler to a point where the heel was sort of half and half on that line. From that position, you would then gauge where his back foot lands. And you draw a line where his back foot lands to act as a guide. If he gets over that line, it's going to be a no-ball, and you just call it so.

In a bid to remain as cordial as possible, you would tell the bowler and try to work with him before it got to that point. Providing advice like 'You're getting close, you're getting close, you are too tight'. If they were unable to adjust after that you would just call it, whether it was a no-ball or not.

Then, if there was any questioning of the decision, the conversation with the player in question might go something like this:

'Now then. You are perhaps going to ask me for something at that end soon. At the moment, you are too tight on this this this line here, so let's work together, get you back a bit and when "soon" comes we might both be happy. Catch my drift?'

It wouldn't work these days because of all the cameras. They are talking millimetres now and people still criticise when borderline no-balls are missed. That's harsh on the work that umpires do, it really is. They often can't see, as I've explained, and that's usually because they have taken up a more withdrawn vantage point upon the request of a bowler.

If you want to apply the law as it reads, the umpire has to stand in a position from which he can see every event. Now, the only place he can do that is right up to the stumps. Right up. Which is not the place to be to get the best view of the far end but allows you to look up and down at the front foot landing from a much closer perspective.

The other thing is, at the start of a four-day game, if you say to this big strapping lad: 'I'm going to stand here, right up at the stumps, because then I can see your front foot', you might have upset him straight away. And then you might do it with the opposition, and you've upset all of them. So standing where bowlers want you to be, as a courtesy, is so much better for everyone.

Norman Gifford was brilliant in this regard. Norman, a left-arm spinner, would curve his run in front of the umpire, and most of the time you knew where you were with him. You had to give him sufficient room to get through the gap from his starting position to your right when he was bowling his stock round-the-wicket stuff.

Norman was a top, top bloke. One of the very best on the circuit. But he could get exasperated and would go redder and redder if things weren't going for him. He'd get a bit fruity at times like these, and when he did, he would start fiddling about with his approach to the crease. He would want to make more space for his run in between you and the stumps.

'Can you go further back? You need to move. Can you get further back?'

I would say: 'Norman, I'm gonna be with the f***ing sawdust here.'

On one occasion, he told me: 'Don't worry, I will tell you when I have overstepped.'

You couldn't make it up. Trouble was, Norman was unusual as a left-arm spinner because he didn't just meander to the crease, or have a little step and a skip into his delivery stride, he had a proper run-up and that made him more liable to push that front line. But he would be very defensive about it.

If you told him: 'Norman, you're right tight,' he'd be straight back with: 'Don't be bothering looking at this end. Concentrate on what's going on down there.'

A long-serving county cricketer with Worcestershire, he won back-to-back championships in the 1960s and another in the '70s, then at the end of his career he moved to Warwickshire, where he was captain.

He was effectively understudy to Derek Underwood for England throughout the majority of his career but he would get in ahead of him every now and again and, despite having a seven-year gap between caps at one juncture, he collected 15 of them in all.

The most extraordinary story of all with him, though, came during his time at Edgbaston. He was 43 when he made his debut for Warwickshire, and would play on until 1988 when he was 48. In the middle of this five-year span, he actually made his one-day international debut. It was at a tournament called the Rothmans Four-Nations Cup in 1984–85, held in Sharjah. David Gower was rested and that meant Gifford was named captain. England lost both their matches, against Australia and Pakistan, but Giff showed that he still had the ability in the second game when he took four wickets, including the prize scalp of Imran Khan first ball. He never played again.

A product of uncovered pitches, like Underwood, he bowled slow left-arm at a briskish pace before adapting to the use of covers later in his career by bringing flight and greater variations of pace into his bowling.

A reflection of his success in doing so was shown in a fabulous first-class career record of 2,068 wickets at 23.56 runs each. Not since 1988 has a player retired with such a volume and the way the modern game has gone, it is almost certain they never will again.

I first came across Barrie Meyer – who was a professional footballer for Bristol Rovers and Bristol City – in the Gloucestershire side that also boasted Arthur Milton, the dual international and twelfth and last individual to be capped by England at football and cricket. As an outside-right, he made a solitary appearance against Austria at Wembley in 1951, and then, after several times as 12th man, his Test debut in 1958.

What a career Milton had. Such an affectionate bloke; as fit as a fiddle, he later kept greyhounds. No wonder he never put weight on. What I recall most fondly about him, however, when I came up against him as a direct opponent in the 1960s, was his willingness to help a young kid like me, making my way in the game.

He would come up and talk to teenage cricketers like myself about batting and bowling in his distinctively strong south-western accent, and there would be lots of 'well dones'. He was great at encouraging you.

Another absolute stalwart of Gloucestershire cricket was David Shepherd. He had simple pleasures, such as his devotion to his county club, and North Devon, where he had played in his youth.

He wouldn't have an enemy in the world and was so respected by players during 22 years of service as an international umpire.

Of course, he had that game where he fell foul of missing the no-balls, against Pakistan at Old Trafford in 2001. It would have been a travesty if he had followed through with his threat to retire following post-match criticism for failing to spot that off-spinner Saqlain Mushtaq had overstepped for three dismissals in an England defeat.

He was mortified as he would not want the game he loved wronged. But, as I have logged, if you can't see, you can't give, and unlike the young technical chaps in the TV trucks who get a side-on camera angle and an exposed view of the whitewash, he did not have the benefit of replays.

Shep was a first-class citizen, both in life and of the sport he served, and his great on-field manner earned him such a good reputation.

CHAPTER 9

The Commentary Box

In December 2019, the world of cricket lost one of the greatest men I've ever met, someone who would do anything for you. The life and soul of any party. Very few would believe it from his television persona but Bob Willis could be outrageous.

In broadcasting, as in cricket, some people have to adapt to less glamorous roles. Think of the hard yards a seamer might have to do on an unresponsive pitch to support the spinner at the other end, or a batsman digging in against the new ball. Well, Bob did that with his work for Sky Sports. Truth is he was nothing like the grumpy sod he portrayed so well on screen. People labelled him 'boring, boring Bob'. They were a million miles from the reality.

Bob was hail-fellow-well-met and at the hub of things socially. Fun happened around him. For example, on a tour of the Caribbean he once got chucked out of a quiz that he himself had organised. He was ejected for swearing.

And he loved socializing, whether it be over a pint or a glass of wine. He was equally happy in pub company or high-brow pursuits such as the opera, and you could find him listening to Bob Dylan or Wagner. As a party piece, he could recite every single word of every song that Dylan ever sang.

In a tribute to his idol, he also changed his name by deed poll, which suited his day job just fine. Robert George Willis became Robert George Dylan Willis and as he acknowledged: 'To be captain of England in those days, you had to have three initials. So I had to add another one, didn't I?'

Our career paths crossed as players, but it was during our broadcasting that he became a true friend. A few years ago, myself, Bob and Paul Allott went on a walking and steam train holiday to the Welsh Highland Railway line that runs from Blaenau Ffestiniog to Porthmadog. It turns out Allott would go down there in his school holidays, clean these steam trains and drive on the footplate.

While he was the aficionado, it was Bob who would do a lot of the organising: 'This is where we're staying, that's the time we will go and catch the train to go there.' And so on.

So we got in this first-class compartment on one of these steam trains, which comprised some nice curtains, a couple of circular tables, with four chairs at each. There was a fellow just sat on his own at one and the other was empty, so we sat down at it and in a flash Bob's got the wine out. As he distributed the glasses, he said to our new travelling companion: 'Would you care to join us?'

After accepting the offer with a 'thank you very much', the following conversation took place:

Bob: Where are you travelling from?

Bloke: I've come up from London.

Bob: Are you local, though? You don't sound like you're from London.

Bloke: Yes, I'm local.

Bob: Have you been down there on business?

Bloke: Yes, well, you could call it that.

Bob: What have you been doing, then, if you don't mind me asking?

Bloke: Not at all. I've been meeting an accountant.

Bob: Oh, that all sounds a very serious business.

Bloke: Yes. It is rather. I've just won the National Lottery . . .

So we toasted his success before disembarking for the first of our walks. This particular one being two miles or so. And Bob is off, as if intent on setting a new record time for the distance. I had to run to keep up with him at the best of times. Here, he's off, through a stile, and charging into an open field.

'Just leave him,' said Walt. 'Let him go.'

So he was yomping across the grass, past a herd of cows and he got to the other side and realised that we weren't there. In fact, we were not anywhere near him.

And so he shouted back to Paul John Walter Allott: 'Come on, Walter, keep up!'

To which Walt cupped his hands to his face and yelled: 'You're going the wrong f***ing way!'

If only Sky had chosen to film it. It would have been a classic *Last of the Summer Wine* sketch. This gangling figure striding vigorously across the field, having failed in his bid to lead. A Foggy to his companions Compo and Cleggy.

As good as he was as a fast bowler, he was always a bit ungainly, yet the funny thing was that whenever you got talking to him about his action and his limbs flailing everywhere, he would reveal that when he first saw himself on television replays he didn't believe it was him. Why? Because he truly believed he sported an action like that of Fred Trueman. A classical side-on affair. One for the aesthetes. But, as the saying goes, 'The camera doesn't lie.'

Neither would Trueman have been flattered by the comparison. I was once on air with Fred on *Test Match Special,* towards the end of Willis's career, when, after watching the bowler's customary first movement in the direction of mid-off before charging down the hill at Headingley, he said: 'He is the only bloke I've ever known that runs away from the wicket before he bowls!'

But Willis had a real talent for bowling fast. All these parts somehow worked in unison and when he was 'on' he was ferocious. And he tried to ensure he was 'on' when it came to international engagements.

Central contracts are fairly familiar to cricket fans of this era, who are used to players being rested for certain periods, kept fresh by rotating matches or being sent off for a family break. Well, Willis used to have his own central contract. He stored it in his head.

At a time when players tended to put their counties first (they were the paymasters, after all) he viewed himself as an England cricketer, and that meant that when he played for

Warwickshire he throttled back, just as John Snow would when he turned out for Sussex.

Every now and again, when it was required, he'd flipping fire up but he couldn't do it every day. It just wasn't physically possible for a fast bowler involved in such heavy county cricket scheduling to crank up to full tilt daily, and so it meant this only happened when it really mattered – be it a decisive Championship match or the latter stages of a knockout one-day cup.

As an opening batsman, I can attest that he wasn't always at optimum speed. Equally, I played against him in a knockout game when he was. Think Allan Donald pace. So I knew the difference. But he was sensible. He knew that if he had a Test match coming up, he couldn't be rattling through a load of overs with the bear and ragged staff on his jumper. So it would be for a concentrated period only.

His body wasn't going to get any protection from those in authority, so he had to protect it himself and it shows he was a cricketer of great intelligence. One who kept himself ready for the big moments.

Others knew it, too. Take Big Jim at Edgbaston, with his cries of: 'Come on, Willis, show us your England form!'

He could certainly steam in. Just look at the 1981 Ashes and the number of times batters are jumping and hopping around. At that time, he was in the zone. And the revelation of how he got there was eye-opening. He said that before he went onto the field he would make a phone call and get hypnotised. Which explains the glazed look on his face beneath that unkempt bush of hair when he was decimating Australia in that epic heist at Headingley in particular.

One of his regrets came in the interview he gave after that match when he had a pop at the media. But in his defence, he just wasn't there. He was talking to Peter West but he was transfixed in some other zone. Absolutely gone.

He could cause some serious bodily harm with ball in hand yet he was such a gentle soul. On the field, he was a competitive beast who, in a one-on-one battle – as exemplified by Headingley – wasn't going to give up until it was over.

He prolonged his career by looking after himself but even then, when he did finish up he was absolutely spent. The key to bowling fast over a 15-year period, he said, was road running – pounding the streets, getting mileage into the legs. Yes, it blitzed his knees, and he had both operated on, but he developed great stamina and when he was pumping into the crease those knees used to get right up to his waist.

Bounce was a major weapon for him and that was produced from those long levers. As a batter, he was one of those bowlers you felt was coming straight at you as soon as he set off from his mark. He ran a long way, too, so the anticipation of receiving the delivery also played a part. Then, his front foot would rise and the ball was being thrust upon you from a great height. Standing at 6ft 6, that meant it was coming down from about nine foot.

This guy wasn't only an England great but a global one. For example, upon entering retirement in 1984, only Dennis Lillee had claimed more than Willis's 325 Test wickets, which came his way at a cost of 25.2 runs apiece. That puts his abilities into context. What indomitable national service.

Sir Ian Botham, so often the provider of the frills and flair to Willis's sweat and graft, dubbed him the one world-class bowler he had played alongside for England. On the occasion of England's 1,000th Test in August 2018, he was named in the country's greatest Test XI by the ECB.

If his sense of game management made him two players, the split in his broadcast duties was between reality and the act he put on. As a pundit, he became someone else whenever filming started for Sky Sports' show The Verdict. And the players drafted in to appear alongside him in the studio in Isleworth from time to time got to realise this. Lads like Steve Harmison, Jimmy Anderson and Stuart Broad would previously have had a bit of a downer on Bob. Until they met him. Then, like the rest of us, they would acknowledge what a great bloke he was.

Perhaps his voice wasn't perfect for commentary. But he could always be trusted to deliver his opinions in a 'tell-it-as-it-is' fashion. There was no flannel.

His reputation as knocker masked the truth. Because what we, his Sky colleagues, knew only too well was that he was desperate for England to be successful. Equally, he had a job to do and he became more outrageous as time passed, often egged on by his sidekick Charles Colvile, nailing their shoddiest performances with relish.

At times he was like a Dickensian villain and his line during the 5-0 whitewash by Australia in the 2013–14 Ashes is legendary.

'They should send them all home. Economy class. And strap some of them to the wings,' he said, delivering the words while looking maniacally into the camera.

He played the irascible role to a tee and so, even when England won, as they did in painstaking manner against New Zealand at Headingley, he came out with: 'There should be three sets of stocks in the town square in Leeds. One for Andy Flower, one for Alastair Cook and one for Jonathan Trott, and there should be a great big barrel of rotten tomatoes to hurl at them.'

It became a bit of a cult thing, The Verdict, and two words prepared you for what was coming next. Coupled together you knew there was going to be some hostility. It was like the fast bowler setting up a batsman. The catchphrase was like a bouncer, setting things up, and what would follow would be the equivalent of a deadly yorker.

'Well, Charles,' he would begin, drawing out each vowel. From that moment you knew that somebody was gonna get absolutely nailed. Just as they were when those eyes glazed over and he pushed off the sight screen from the Kirkstall Lane end.

His spleen was not only vented upon the players, though. Take his first visit to Canterbury, after the violent winter storms of 2004–05, when Charlie said: 'Isn't it awful, Bob, that the old lime tree is now gone?'

'It should have been chopped down years ago,' came the deadpan reply. 'Whoever heard of a tree in the middle of a cricket ground?'

He got booed on the way to his car by the Kent members after that and so, in response, within the first five minutes of every subsequent commentary stint at the St Lawrence Ground, he would chime in with: 'They've always been a one-eyed lot here.'

Then there was the antagonism he created when asked by

Charlie: 'What do you think of the Barmy Army?' and without hesitation, replied: 'They should all be gassed.'

Hence their 'boring, boring Bob Willis' song.

But he wasn't looking for grace or favour. As he showed when he gave Chris Woakes a mark of zero when asked to rate the players out of 10. It ended up with him having to write a letter of apology to Woakes, one of the nicest guys the cricket world's ever seen.

But Bob had been adamant: 'I can't give him a point just for turning up.'

It would have given him no pleasure seeing an England player struggle. It did bother him that he was viewed in a certain way by some, but he just accepted that his duty as a pundit was to provide opinion.

Some people called him Chainsaw Bob. But to those who got to know him, Air Guitar Bob would have been more apt – because if you want evidence of this snarl being an act, have a search on YouTube and you will find him strumming his imaginary instrument in the commentary box.

Naturally shy and slightly withdrawn, nothing excited him more than seeing a new fast bowler emerge. He would be willing them all to do well and he was absolutely thrilled for Jimmy Anderson when he got to 500 Test wickets – the kid who had so impressed him all those years earlier during a televised 2002 county match versus Somerset.

Pressing the lazy switch, he asked: 'Is that speed gun correct? This kid's bowling at ninety miles an hour.'

Yeah, it's fine, mate.

'F*** me!'

That was the kind of thing to get him excited. He was also very analytical with his criticism, always trying to put into context where players had gone wrong in a straightforward, sometimes abrupt manner. Let's just say he wouldn't go round the houses to get to the town.

'This chap's not very good.'

Don't mince your words, Bob.

Away from 'work', as Steve Harmison among others was to discover, he was great company. And a fan of social gatherings.

Towards the end of every English season, you'd get a call. 'I think we should have a particularly long lunch,' would be the suggestion.

Turn up and you would find an eclectic mix from inside and outside sport. He just had a knack of pulling people together and having a bloody good time.

He was a great all-round sportsman – goalkeeper for Corinthian Casuals and not a bad tennis player, who always wore a trilby like Fred Perry. He was at Wimbledon every year. The anomaly was golf.

Despite playing weekly, his handicap was 19, and it's fair to say I've never heard somebody scream so much over 18 holes.

'Do you know, there are times when I don't even know that I've hit the bloody thing,' Bob would say.

His swing? Well, if you ever saw him when he was batting . . . Of course, he walked out without a bat one game. He just had no co-ordination.

When in New Zealand, we try to play golf at Paraparaumu

just outside Wellington, which is one of the country's great courses.

Straight away, Beefy states: 'Right then, we're all playing off the blacks. We haven't come all this way to play off them girly tees.'

To the uninitiated, that meant we were playing off the championship tees, not the usual club ones. Well, it was blowing an absolute hooley and Bob couldn't reach the fairway!

In contrast, Botham gave his ball a ferocious smite, sending it careering into the clubhouse and rebounding off the windows as if in a pinball machine.

He was always up for adventure, Bob. On one tour of Bangladesh, we had four days off and Paul Allott vowed to teach the two of us how to play bridge. However, it soon became clear that 96 hours of tuition from Miss Allott, as Bob christened him that week, was over-optimistic and so we required other pursuits.

Opposite our hotel – the luxurious-sounding Agra, which was anything but – there was a light that pricked Bob's curiosity. Wandering over, he discovered it was not what you might be thinking but a travel agent.

Keen for an excursion, he walked in and enquired: 'Tell me, where have you got a direct flight to?'

'Where would you like to go?'

'Anywhere.'

It was just a one-and-a-half-hour direct flight to Thailand and so we ended up going to Chiang Mai for three days, took our golf clubs and played under floodlights. It may also be true that we frequented a place called the Lucky Bar. My memory is a bit hazy . . .

Broadcasting has offered a rich second career and I will always be indebted to Peter Baxter, the long-standing producer of *Test Match Special*, for taking me on and giving me a chance on the radio at a vintage time. The *TMS* cast in the 1980s included Brian Johnston, Fred Trueman, Don Mosey, Trevor Bailey, Christopher Martin-Jenkins, Bill Frindall, Henry Blofeld and a young Jonathan Agnew. We had an enormous amount of fun.

A glass of wine throughout the day didn't go amiss and Fred was hilarious with one or without. One of my all-time heroes as an on-field competitor, to work alongside him was a privilege. He couldn't have been a more archetypal Yorkshireman.

Sometimes it would take him ages to get it going but his pipe would billow like Ferrybridge Power Station, and it would prove a nightmare for the rest of us if the wind was blowing in the wrong direction.

Invariably, Fred was late for duty. Even for games on his own patch at Headingley. Picture this: we are in the old commentary box at the ground, which is really no more than an 8ft x 6ft shed. On this particular occasion, Johnners has already started the first commentary stint of the live action.

'Oh, Fred's arrived!' he declares on air. 'Marvellous to see you, Fred. Have you been stuck in traffic?'

'Trouble parking car, Brian. But I'm here now.'

Referring to the smoking of his pipe, Johnners said: 'You don't inhale, do you?'

Right on cue, up pops Frindall, the Bearded Wonder, with: 'No, but we do!'

Within a couple of minutes we couldn't see a thing out of the window. The entire box had been consumed by a fog of Condor Twist.

Johnston was always trying to wind up Trueman for the delectation of the listener. Particularly when a young Darren Gough arrived on the scene in the 1990s.

'Isn't it exciting that Yorkshire have unearthed this young chap?' he would tease. 'He certainly looks like the fastest bowler from Yorkshire since the war.'

'You what? I can bowl faster than that in a mac and a pair of wellingtons.'

Infected with a chronic dose of hubris, Fred would fall into the trap every time.

These were the days of the fax machine, and myself and Jonathan Agnew, the two newest kids on the *TMS* block, used to send spoofs in pretending to be listeners. We would send them in and Henry Blofeld would read them out.

At one Test match at Edgbaston, he began: 'I wonder if you can help. We are a social cricket team from the West Country on tour in the local area. We're in the Cotswolds and we know that our scorer Ted Cornthwaite is a spectator at the ground today. But he will be keeping himself to himself. In fact, he's very shy, so he will be sat on his own. Sorry to trouble you but we are appealing to him as he has got the balls in the boot of his car and we can't start this afternoon's game without him.'

In wades Blowers.

'If you're out there, Shy Ted, we need your balls.'

Another Blowers set-up played on his love of a freebie. It was supposedly from such-and-such a carpet shop.

'We're all listening, and we are cricket mad,' was the gist.

'It would be great if you could give us a mention. If you managed it, there would be a free carpet coming your way.'

Blofeld: 'Campbell's Carpets are listening, marvellous to have you with us.'

During the same Test match, Agnew sends in another from a company claiming to be Campbell's local competitors, threatening to report Blowers to the Broadcasting Standards Commission.

'I'm terribly sorry,' Blowers told the listeners. 'Of course, I neglected to mention earlier that there are other carpet manufacturers available.'

There were serious aspects to the programme, of course. For example, I would marvel at Don Mosey and how he would summarise at the end of a day's play. He would just stare at the pitch and be word-perfect in recollection of what had happened over the previous seven hours. No notes, nothing.

But it was a real hoot, too, and Johnston would lead the charge, both on air and after play. 'We will be having dinner at such and such a place this evening,' he would say. He never booked ahead but he was such a commanding bloke – standing at six and a half feet and a former Grenadier Guard, of course – that room was regularly found for us. He would open the door to make a grand entrance, people would recognise him and he would confidently enquire: 'Is it the usual table in the corner?' It seemed to work every time.

The classic off-air story involving Johnners was when Fred's daughter Rebecca married Raquel Welch's son, Damon, at St Mary's and St Cuthbert's in the summer of 1991.

'How did the wedding go, Fred? It must have been a wonderful occasion at Bolton Abbey.'

Fred: 'Magnificent, it was a wonderful day, Brian, lad.'

In true American actress-style, Welch had turned up in a chauffeur-driven Mercedes, emerging from the vehicle fashionably late with bodyguards in tow. Afterwards, there was a six-course meal at the Devonshire Arms pub next door.

'Did you meet Raquel? What sort of a lady was she?'

'Skin like porcelain, at fifty years of age. Would you credit it? Not a bloody wrinkle anywhere on her face. She looked magnificent. Magnificent. She had a dress on that were down 'ere, like that, and up 'ere, like that,' pointing to his chest and his legs. 'Ooh, I've got thicker belts than that dress.'

Johnners comes back with: 'I was rather thinking what sort of personality she was, Fred.'

It was to prove a fleeting alliance and as Trueman himself said: 'That marriage didn't last as long as my run-up.'

Always capable of a cracking delivery was Fred. Take his reaction to Neil Mallender's Test debut versus Pakistan in Leeds in 1992.

'There are some great bowlers to have run in from the Kirkstall Lane end,' Fred reminisced, before delivering the punchline, 'and he's not one of them!'

Adding: 'Furthermore, he doesn't look a well man to me.' His nickname was Ghostie by virtue of his rather sallow complexion.

For the record, the Yorkshire-born Mallender had been a horses-for-courses pick in conditions that favoured seam movement. Five wickets in the second innings and an eight-wicket match haul suggested Fred had been a tad harsh.

But it was vintage radio commentary. *Test Match Special* became an institution and attracted some unusual behaviour from its devotees. I once did an after-dinner speech in Bishop's Stortford and the club chairman met me with his wife. His wife told me that they were avid listeners.

'That's lovely,' I told them.

'Yes, when it comes on, John puts his umpire's jacket on and creosotes the fence.'

'He does what?'

She said: 'He takes the radio and paints the fence all day.'

'Well, what happens when it rains?' I asked.

'He loves it,' she said. 'He gets in the car and has a drive round the M25. He thinks it's even better when there's no play – and everybody's just having a chat.'

One of the most famous moments in *TMS* history came during an end-of-innings summary between Brian Johnston and Jonathan Agnew at the 1991 Oval Test match versus West Indies. Despite descending into hysterical giggles, Johnners did not like playing his part in the Ian Botham leg-over moment until persuaded by his radio teammates that people had loved it.

'He tried to do the splits over it and unfortunately the inner part of his thigh must have just removed the bail,' Johnston said of Botham's hit-wicket dismissal on the second day.

'He just didn't quite get his leg over,' Agnew interjected, triggering the sniggering.

Thankfully everyone saw the funny side. Which wasn't true when Botham himself was summarising the fourth day's play of England's contest versus India at Lord's in 2007 for a Sky Sports video blog.

In a studio in the media centre, he is communicating with the outside broadcast truck and there is a sequence of pictures that is being played to back up his words. Only the sequence is all wrong.

'The best day of the summer so far . . . Kevin Pietersen, his ninth Test hundred,' Beefy says, before unleashing a volley of expletives as he realises pictures of the umpires inspecting the ground with brollies up and the full square covered are the backdrop. It was absolutely pissing down.

Then, on the next take, he ends up looking at the wrong camera so he's offset and on a screen behind him emerges Dave, one of the cameramen, whose job it is to detach the microphone daily.

The director clearly gives him word of what has happened and that they will have to stop again.

Beefy's getting thirsty by this time and he wants to get off.

'What the f***'s going on?' he demands.

So, anyway, they persist and are on about take five when he says, 'Kevin Pietersen has got his name on . . . got his name on . . . got his name on the . . .' clearly having forgotten what it's called. He's started playing a game of charades, making a square in the air with his hands, signalling like an umpire doing a review, until he gets word in his ear again: HONOURS BOARD.

Of course, he has to do it all again. Beefy is like Vesuvius and a group of us are in the next room watching it develop in floods of tears. Paul King, our boss at the time, later got everybody together to reinforce that nobody was to mention this episode to anyone, ever.

But as he's no longer our boss and Beefy is no longer our colleague, I reckon the amnesty is over.

Beefy and David Gower left Sky in 2019 after two decades of service. I always thought my favourite Gower moment was going to be his classic handover disaster with Nasser Hussain in the Brisbane Ashes Test of 2010–11 when he got up out of his seat and leant out of the way as Nasser picks up his own chair, plonks it straight down on Gower's foot and sits on it.

There was a sharp shriek into the microphone like someone had been shot. Lord Gower is usually as smooth as you like. Not on this occasion. He can't move. His foot has been pinned to the floor, and he walks with a limp for the rest of the Test match.

But he of the magisterial presenting style trumped it in his final throes when, during his last Test with Sky, the fifth Ashes Test of 2019 at The Oval, he was involved in a bit of a faux pas. He was throwing back to the commentary from the studio and it would have been on a note somewhere who the next two commentators would be. Unfortunately, he clearly could not see it and so all you could hear at the conclusion of his introduction to them was 'and the next two commentators are . . .' was a muffled silence, followed by: 'I've no f***ing idea who they are.'

When something like this happens, as an organisation you have got to apologise straight away, which Shane Warne did.

But nobody died. It was a mistake, and when you cock up in live broadcasting you've got to add some perspective. In such circumstances, we get a circular email reminding us that microphones are live all the time but the lowering of the Gower guard did nothing to harm his cult status judging by the piss-taking on Twitter about him being a potty mouth.

Sky have got two absolute gems in Michael Atherton and Nasser Hussain, two other former England captains who know the game inside out. I realised what great game brains they had when I was coach of England during the 1990s.

Atherton was always destined to be Future England Captain. He carried around that nickname as an outstanding schoolboy cricketer, and then got into senior captaincy by leading a Combined Universities team, including Hussain and Steve James, to within four runs of the semi-final stage of the 1989 Benson & Hedges.

A real thinker and tactician of the game, he was a great believer in individuals taking responsibility within the team environment. His big phrase was 'do your job'.

As an opening batsman, he was one of the bravest, taking over that Geoffrey Boycott mantra of 'over my dead body, you're gonna get me out'. He loved a battle out there on the field but crucially he could *leave* it out there on the field.

There was no better example of this than the duel he had with Allan Donald at Trent Bridge during the 1998 series between England and the South Africans. It was feisty throughout what would turn out to be England's first victory in a series of five matches or greater in five years. No quarter asked, nor given.

Now at that time his back condition was not good at all, so when Donald hurled hellfire at him – incensed by having a glove through from Atherton to Mark Boucher on 27 not given – it meant a really uncomfortable passage of play lay ahead. Having had a metal plate inserted, he couldn't actually duck the barrage of bouncers that followed, as he would ideally have liked. So he either had to sway out of the way of deliveries or take them on. This was something that hindered him throughout his career, big time, and it is why I believe he finished up averaging 37.69 in 118 Tests when he should have been a 45.

His injury, which would flare up at any given moment, really impeded him and he just couldn't do what he wanted to do. Yet he still loved acts of defiance. Again, take the epic 10 hours with Jack Russell as his mate at the other end, to save a game in Johannesburg in 1995 – he absolutely loved that. To save a game is a great challenge, and an underrated one in an age of much higher win ratios for Test cricket.

His public persona as captain was nothing like what he is. His lighter side came out in the dressing-room environment. Yes, there was a ruthless streak to his captaincy. Recall the episode with Graeme Hick when he declared on him in an away Ashes Test when he was on 98. But he was well respected by everybody who played under him. He cared about the welfare of individuals, particularly on tour. He was one of those who could tell when someone was not quite right, and he would go and knock on his door and ask 'Are you okay?'

He's still the same now as a broadcast colleague. Take his

befriending of Pakistan's Mohammad Amir following the spot-fixing saga of 2011. He recognised that this lad had made a mistake, that he was vulnerable and went to great lengths to support him, arranging private meetings to make sure he was all right. He understood the problems that Amir, as a kid, would experience with senior players. My perspective was that he'd done wrong and had been banged to rights but Athers taught me to open my eyes and look deeper than that. That he had been very vulnerable as a young player within that Pakistan team and his elders had preyed upon that vulnerability.

He has done a similar thing to support his former England teammate Chris Lewis following his release from prison. He has a great way about him. He'd make a very good prime minister, and I anticipate a vacancy soon.

Don't get me wrong; he has had his moments, too, and would get the competitive juices flowing by picking a scrap on the field. Never more so than when England played Pakistan in the mid-1990s. A bloke came in to field, close up on the off-side, and Athers reacted by stepping back and warning the umpire: 'If he says another word, I will hit him with the bat.'

Incredulous, the individual in question retaliated: 'I have only just come on, I am twelfth man.'

He had picked the wrong fielder!

Atherton also possessed a wicked sense of humour, never more so than in the West Indies in 1997–98 when Hussain was batting and was dismissed by a pea-roller of a delivery from the off-spinner Carl Hooper in the third Test in

Trinidad. It hit him on the toe and Eddie Nicholls had to keep a straight face and give him out. Ath couldn't, though. Nasser is like Popeye, with steam coming out of his ears, when he gets back into the dressing room. And all Atherton could do was burst out laughing.

These days, Nasser is hugely respected as a deep thinker of the game. Back then, he was very volatile. You never quite knew what was going to happen next with Nasser.

For him it was all practise, practise, practise. There would be zero attention to any fitness – at odds with what he is like now – he just wanted to bat. In fact, he couldn't wait to get batting when it came to nets, and he would think nothing of taking 10 minutes of somebody else's batting time, too, if he could.

His single-mindedness, some might argue selfishness, certainly counted against him when Atherton resigned in 1997. I sat in an EMAC (England Management Advisory Committee) meeting alongside Bob Bennett, Ian MacLaurin, Brian Bolus, Doug Insole and David Acfield, at which the latter two, both from Essex, said: 'On no account think of our bloke!'

That now sounds extraordinary because of what a respected England captain he became. But if you looked at it from a county perspective then he had form, and I am not talking about his statistical returns. He would be hard to handle, would rock the boat with his behaviour from time to time and was so self-driven, the general attitude towards any kind of promotion at Chelmsford would have been met with a 'you must be f***ing joking'.

Keith Fletcher, as captain and then team manager, would

have to leave him out for some misdemeanour on the field. And so that's what they would see.

But when he eventually became captain and developed that great relationship with Duncan Fletcher, who's probably England's best coach, he was known to be a disciplinarian.

They laugh about it now that they are colleagues at Sky but when Rob Key got into England's team in 2002, he was carrying a bit too much timber. Andrew Flintoff was also in the team and Nasser, from mid-off, shouted down to him: 'Key, you fat git, stop talking to your f***ing mate.'

As a captain, he would think out of the box. It wasn't the standard two slips, a gully, a mid-off, when setting fields. He would have the most threatening field for each bowler to each individual batsman worked out, and was always trying to pick out opposition players' weaknesses or potential vulnerabilities, which made him very open to asking a bowler: 'Please, do this.' Or: 'I want you to bowl to this particular field.' Most notably when a tight over-the-wicket line from Ashley Giles resulted in the first stumping of Sachin Tendulkar's Test career on the tour of 2001–02. Tactically, he was as good as England have had in the modern era.

Of course, he retained his headstrong ways. That much could be seen when he stuck three fingers up to the Lord's media centre in a one-day international against India in 2002, having just struck a hundred. That gesture, coupled with the pointing to the number three on the back of his shirt, showed he was never afraid to show his feelings in public. He believed he had shown critics like Botham, Willis and Agnew that he was in his rightful position in the batting order.

That drive to prove people wrong was undoubtedly inherited from his father Joe, who ran an indoor cricket school in Essex. His sister, who is with the Royal Ballet, and brothers have been high achievers, too.

As he was coming through with England, other lads in the squad would complain of the noise he would make in hotel rooms because he would take a bat and ball, and just hit it against the wall, until the wee small hours. They would lay there awake, listening: 'boom, boom, boom'.

It is fair to say age has mellowed him and he has such great clarity of thought on the game these days. Just listen to his key moments when he is talking tactics. When games get down to the wire, or into the last session, there is nobody better among us.

Like a lot of cricketers, he is also an avid weather watcher – when you have done years on the county circuit you are always keen for a bit of rain, a bit of time off – and he has the beak to sniff it out if it's in the air.

Sky Sports has had a new broom sweep through in the last couple of years and one of those promoted for greater responsibilities is Ian Ward. A very accomplished presenter, and a great mate.

He is one I spend a lot of downtime with, making social media video clips together and heading down the pub. Often a combination of the two simultaneously.

One of our favourites is to take off the sort of speak you might get at a cocktail party when two blokes have nothing else to say to each other.

'Hello, Rodney.'

'Hello, Charles.'

'How are you?'

'Fine.'

'Have you seen ... ?'

'No, no, no. I've not. Where's he been?'

'I haven't seen him for a long time?'

'Did you?'

'No, no, no.'

There is nothing of substance said for about 10 minutes.

We filmed one of our sketches in Soho, in front of a shop selling all kinds of unusual paraphernalia. I couldn't tell you the full contents of what was inside but there was certainly a decent range of gimp masks and other fetish gear in the window.

People on Twitter were diving in with: 'Have you realised where you are stood?' Or 'Have a look behind you!'

A discovery. I can play some decent tunes on Wardy's leg. 'Piano Man' by Billy Joel and 'Annie's Song' from John Denver are ones I have got down to a tee. We have also started redoing my old-school Sky Sports' spoof pitch reports. Usually when drink has been taken. Just in case anybody feared I can do them sober.

To some people broadcasting comes naturally. There is no better example than Rob Key. Within a couple of engagements, the people behind the scenes at Sky were saying: 'This bloke's bloody brilliant.' It helps that he knows the county game particularly well and he is easy to listen to. He took to punditry like a duck to water. Loves a game of cards, too, which is no bad thing considering we spend so much time travelling in this job.

These new blokes keep me feeling young. Not that age dictates the level of excitement you feel when on commentary. In fact, the person that gave me goosebumps when working with them for the first time was Bill Lawry when I was seconded by Channel 9 for the 2013–14 Ashes.

Totally one-eyed is Bill. There are times when you have to check there are two teams playing and when it comes to his favouritism he is Australian second, Victorian first. Nevertheless, he is a great voice, and possesses enthusiasm like you've never seen, which is incongruous really because he was quite a dour batsman back in the day.

Whenever you heard this bloke commentating on a one-day game that was going to the wire you wouldn't have believed he was in his late seventies. Give me Bill Lawry any day. Fabulous listening.

Paired up with him, you know he could fire off at any moment, and then you've entered his excitable phase. The Melbourne Cricket Ground was rammed and I was just waiting for the moment.

'I tell you what, Bill, this is a half-decent ground, this.'

Like a coiled spring: 'Half-decent ground!?!? This is the G. This is the greatest ground in the world!'

I had done him like a kipper. And when we came off air he acknowledged it with a 'loved that!'

It was also the kind of fun jape of which Bob Willis would have approved. Especially getting one over on an Australian. You see, despite making a career of this, a lot of his best mates were actually Aussies, and he adored the country.

CHAPTER 10

The Tracksuit

Relationships you develop with players as a coach are quite different from those with fellow teammates, and so when those you have helped on their journey succeed, it provides an inevitable sense of pride. For me this was the case with Andrew Flintoff.

I first met him when he was still at school and Northamptonshire were offering him the chance to finish his education privately as part of a package for him to join their playing staff. Myself and Geoff Ogden, Lancashire's chairman of cricket in the early 1990s, put the case for him staying where he was and signing forms for his home county.

As a cricketer, he was always a natural entertainer. A batsman who could hit the ball into the middle of next week, a launcher of Exocets as a bowler and a fielder with two huge scoops for hands. It was obvious from the age of 16 that this lad could be anything he wanted to be. There was no ceiling to what he could achieve, and for a three-year period he fulfilled that potential to be recognised as the most devastating all-rounder on the planet.

Although Flintoff played international cricket between 1998 and 2009, it was the period between April 2003 and April 2006 that showed the levels he could achieve when his body held up. During that period, he played 38 of his 79 Tests. His batting average of 41.3 was almost 10 runs better than his career return while his 141 wickets came at 27.78 runs apiece, five runs better than his overall ratio. It was also during this time that he struck all three of his one-day international hundreds. His average was 46.51, an increase of 45 per cent.

Sadly, that proved boom time for a fierce on-field competitor. He didn't come off second best in many on-field skirmishes but the ongoing battle he had off the field with his knee was one he finally succumbed to when injuries forced his England retirement.

Evidence that this lad wasn't going to take a backward step was provided on the England Under-19 tour of Zimbabwe in 1995–96. As coach it was my remit to turn this group of spotty lads into senior cricketers, although some were maturing faster than others.

It was the first week of 1996. Flintoff had celebrated his 18th birthday the previous month and we were playing a Mashonaland representative side in a warm-up match. The hosts had a chap in their team by the name of Craig Evans, and it seemed pretty apparent from his conduct that he considered this kind of fixture to be well beneath him. That same January, he would take his collection of one-day international caps to six, and he would go on to make his Test debut later in the year. In addition to his cricket ability, he was also a good golfer and played rugby union for Zimbabwe to boot. All in all, a bit of a rising sporting star.

When it came to his turn, Evans walked in to bat not from the pavilion but from the stands where he was sat with his mates. Immediately Flintoff, the youngest in our group, confronted him.

'Do you not think we're good enough to play against?'

Youngest he may have been, and asking what was effectively a rhetorical question of a 26-year-old dual international, but he knew all about the ethical code cricket should uphold. Andrew always had something about him in combat. He always respected his opponents. Of all the images that come to mind of his career, the one of him consoling a distraught Brett Lee on the pitch at Edgbaston in the immediate aftermath of England's two-run win in 2005 is prominent.

Back in that winter of 1995–96, Flintoff was an opening batsman. He was focusing on his batting because we had unwittingly overbowled him in his youth. He was such a colossus of a lad, but he suffered through his physical growth. All the bowling built up his back too quickly and so, under medical advice, we had to stop him bowling for a while to try to decelerate the transformation process from a boy to a man. To keep him in adolescence longer, if you like.

It was already obvious that this lad was going to be a seriously good fast bowler. When we got him into Lancashire's first team, Warren Hegg was the established wicketkeeper and had been used to keeping wicket to Wasim Akram for several years. But he came back into the changing room one day, only about a month into Flintoff's spell in the side, aghast. 'I'm standing further back to the kid than I am to Akram,' he said.

In future years with England, once the back issues were a thing of the past, whenever he came on to bowl there was always a real buzz around the ground. The crowd used to build up into a beehive hum in anticipation of something monumental happening.

Few players to have represented England have had such a strong connection with the crowd, in fact. It was a two-way thing. He lifted the crowd and they lifted him. What a feeling it must be to know that 20,000-odd people are right behind you. It is a special bond to have. Cricket fans are not daft and British ones want one thing in a player more than anything else – effort. They will take that over results every time if they know you are putting in 100 per cent.

During the epic 2005 Ashes it was an enthralling sight as he steamed in to bowl. If you were trying to categorise his bowling it would not have been quick. He was rapid. Think of 12 on the Beaufort scale. This was the year he was in his absolute prime and was a member of the best bowling attack England have ever put together. What a handful Matthew Hoggard, Steve Harmison, Flintoff, Simon Jones and Ashley Giles proved to be.

As well as being able to 'slip himself' – the bowler's term for producing an extra yard of pace at the drop of a hat – Flintoff knew when it was his time. He knew the moment.

He won't like it to be said because he saw himself as a batter, but his devastating effects for England were with the ball.

There was no doubt he was a genuine all-rounder, and someone who could change the course of a game with the bat. But he influenced results with the ball. He was not someone who took five-fors. In fact, he only took three in his entire Test career but you had that sense that when he was on it with the ball, something was going to happen and you couldn't take your eyes off the theatre he created. And the pace he produced was relentless.

Before he slipped off into Test retirement he gave us one last reprise of his undoubted gifts in that unbelievably hostile spell versus Australia in 2009, in which he completed the third and final one of his five-wicket hauls. It was no coincidence, I thought, that the venue for this was Lord's, cricket's most famous gallery and a place at which he had such a huge well of support behind him.

The whole country was willing him on and Andrew Strauss got everything out of him as captain.

Flintoff was one of those players who had a great feel for sense of occasion. It's why his best performances often came against Australia. He shone when the limelight was at its brightest.

Of course, it was when he was suffering most with his knee pain that he produced one of the great moments of Ashes cricket, running out Ricky Ponting at The Oval in the decisive match of that 2009 series. As soon as Mike Hussey clipped the ball to the leg-side, I moved forward in my seat. I had great vision of the batsmen setting off for a tight single and Flintoff running around to his left, and swooping at mid-on, to unleash his slingshot throw. In a flash, a stump was flattened at the batsman's end and Ponting was gone.

I had done exactly the same as a spectator in a NatWest Bank knockout match at Old Trafford between Lancashire and Yorkshire in 1998. Darren Lehmann was a gun player and Yorkshire's greatest threat, one of the best batters that Yorkshire ever had. Naturally, a lot of discussion in the home side's tactics meeting had been based around how they were going to get him out, and I know from talking to my son Graham that they had focused on the fact that he was not the greatest behind the wickets. It was to be kept in mind that he was a run-out victim waiting to happen.

And so it came to pass, when Lehmann pushed into the covers and took Graham on. I was sitting in the pavilion square on, and as soon as ball hit bat on that occasion it was like a reflex to follow what would happen next. I punched the air as the throw hit the stumps. He'd called the run to the wrong fielder.

I was England coach at this time and had received a call from John Abrahams, who had taken over the Under-19s from me in 1996. 'I have got two that are ready to play big boys' cricket,' he told me. The two names he was putting forward for the full England team at the start of the 1997 summer were Ben Hollioake and Andrew Flintoff. Within a year we had got them both in.

People often talk about young players being 'discovered'. There was no discovery necessary for Flintoff. He was established in the school system and was going to be a superstar.

The same in the South-west with Marcus Trescothick. If boys are making eye-catching scores and taking bundles of wickets you know who they are.

Trescothick was captain of England Under-19s in the summer of 1995, having previously played for the team under Michael Vaughan. The problem was that when he went back to trying to establish himself in county cricket he struggled to get into Somerset's team as an opening batsman. During the mid-1990s, when he was an Under-19, he had opened with Mark Lathwell but the county then signed the experienced Peter Bowler at the top of their order, Piran Holloway was another contending for the spot and when Jamie Cox, the prolific Australian, arrived as captain it was a case of too many cooks. It meant Trescothick's only avenue was as a middle-order player who bowled a bit.

When Duncan Fletcher saw him while coaching Glamorgan to the 1999 Championship title, he made a judgement call, and a shrewd one, but prior to him doing so it wasn't as though we had just let things ride. As an England management group we were perturbed that he hadn't been pushing on. In the time before central contacts came in, however, we had our hands tied. He was Somerset's player and as such what they did with him was up to them. Dermot Reeve had struggled to get him in. So, although Duncan deserves credit for his England selection it only really happened because of the power of central contracts. Suddenly, the ECB could influence which games players played for their counties. And could request the role they wished players to play.

Like Trescothick, Flintoff was a game-changer with a great

on-field presence. He was a rollicking character in his early days. He was always going to be a superstar. It took a little bit of time for him to find his feet, partly because he enjoyed himself and arguably enjoyed himself too much, partly because he had to work out when he needed to eliminate enjoying himself, but that was when he was a young lad and eventually he got there. His wife, Rachael, has been great for him and my theory is that she just let him spend his twenties burning himself out.

He was so frustrated and angry that injuries were holding him back – and they finished his career prematurely, of course – that he sought solace in alcohol. A number of us who had known him throughout his time as a player, starting in Lancashire's youth teams, were worried about him. Thankfully, with good people around him, he found some stability; there is no doubt, though, that as a young man he found dealing with adversity difficult. As he recognised that his career was hurtling towards its end, it hurt him and his reaction to it was that he decided he no longer liked cricket. Of course, he did. That was just frustration talking. The injuries and his retirement from England had taken their toll on him.

These days, he's a changed man. Still very affectionate but a teetotaler who has found a different way of entertaining his audience. He seems fulfilled as a television presenter on *A League of Their Own* and *Top Gear* and it is good that he will put this experience to use by returning to cricket to present The Hundred. He is the kind of character that cricket needs to project itself positively.

Unfortunately, we lost another such character from this

category too soon. As I mentioned, Ben Hollioake came through when I was England coach and his international debut against Australia at Lord's in 1997 was one I will never forget. Alec Stewart was captain and when we picked him, we were very strong in the belief that we should shove him in at three, to allow him to express himself in the manner he had been doing for Surrey, rather than leave him down at number seven.

He announced himself to a wider audience by smacking Glenn McGrath and Jason Gillespie in an innings of 63 off just 48 balls. Once he had established himself – all young players need time – he would have been a box-office cricketer. He was very much still learning when he died at the age of 24 in 2002. Had England been able to pair him and Flintoff together, it would have been a fabulous era and the one-day peak we saw between 2015 and 2019 would have arrived much earlier without a doubt, because, with the bit of cricket maturity a couple more years would have given him, Hollioake junior could have been anything he wanted. Quite simply, he had a bit of everything. He could bowl at a lively pace, field as well as anyone you've ever seen, was a quick runner and would give it a smack with the bat.

He was different from his older brother Adam in that he was a little bit more passive. Then again, Adam would have clambered into a ring with Mike Tyson thinking he could win, so he was different from most. Adam Hollioake was a rollicking, raucous lad whose forte was one-day cricket and he played cricket like it was a street fight. It came as no surprise to me that he turned to mixed martial arts post-cricket.

Adam's top-level skill was bowling, really, with the white ball at the end of a game. He was an absolute box of tricks with his spread fingers, the use of the crease to create different angles, slower balls, yorkers. As a captain there was a push towards inventive fields and extreme fitness. Aggression and athleticism were key ingredients for his teams in the field. He was a market leader in one-day innovation, and I can only think he would have gone for a pretty penny at Indian Premier League auctions had he been in his prime in the second decade of the 21st century.

Characters like him, who care little for reputations and live by a what-you-see-is-what-you-get attitude have always intrigued me but cricket teams are made up of lots of other types, too, and it is with regret that I say that I never got to know another Surrey all-rounder in Chris Lewis. I felt as if there was no time to get to know him. He seemed quite a complex character, had a lot going on in his life and it's a big disappointment to me that I never formed any sort of relationship with him. I always thought that he was a bit wary of me. Arguably that was to do with my position of authority as England coach and so I left Michael Atherton and Alec Stewart, who had played a lot of cricket with him prior to my appointment and with whom Stewie had played alongside at county level, to deal with him.

Make no mistake, this lad was a complete cricketer. What an athlete. As fantastic an athlete as has been in the game of cricket. If there has been a better physique, it has been well concealed.

Those injury niggles he used to pick up were a source of

frustration because, if you look at the skill, he was an incredible and ultimately unfulfilled talent. He bowled close to the wicket and, not just because of the Caribbean background, I see so much of him in Jofra Archer. From a point of release nice and tight into the stumps, he would make them play, and his bowling on any given day was hellfire. Unfortunately, next day, it would be anything but.

Ken Higgs was his mentor at Leicestershire. Higgs never enthused about anything. He was your archetypal county professional, ready to have a grumble at the drop of a hat. Nothing was ever good. But, boy, he enthused about Lewis.

Not long into my England tenure, there was evidence why. It was a Test match against India at Lord's and, on what was a flat pitch, he bowled an outstanding over to Sachin Tendulkar. Having rapped Tendulkar on the gloves and been hit away for a boundary previously, he produced a delivery to flatten off-stump. It was just brilliant.

He seemed to be one of those bowlers for whom it would click and everything would work in unison. But things had to be absolutely right for him because, as I say, suddenly he'd be injured. Perhaps when his confidence levels dropped, the aches and pains he bowled through through when he was on top form bothered him. Perhaps it was when he was feeling vulnerable. In those days, fast bowlers had little down time. It was county cricket one day, international the next, so there was little respite for the body.

He played in the 1992 World Cup as a batsman despite not being fit enough to bowl. Or would only bowl in an emergency. You've got to be good to do that. The England team of '92 was as good as we had produced in one-day cricket until the one that's emerged these past few years under Eoin Morgan. As a fielder, he moved so serenely; with his combined attributes he should have been a world-class cricketer. He had everything and perhaps would have fulfilled his potential on a central contract.

Unfortunately, later in life he took a wrong turn and spent half of a 13-year sentence in prison for smuggling cocaine into the UK. I sincerely hope that he's all right. I'm a massive believer in second chances. Following his release in 2009, a play of his life story has been made and it appears from what he has said publicly that it has helped him rehabilitate.

Alan Mullally was an absolute beauty. Any more laid-back and he would have been comatose. As a new-ball bowler he had all the right attributes. Other than aggression.

After a run of nine Test matches, starting with the home series of 1996 against India and Pakistan, it was decided on the tour of New Zealand in early 1997 that we would leave him out for the second match. He was such a nice lad and it's never easy to tell anyone they're not playing, which meant I agonised over how to pitch it to him. Typically, when it came to the big moment he just said straight away: 'I expected it. I'm not getting enough wickets.'

His first home summer had been sound in a statistical sense, comprising 22 wickets in six appearances at an average of 30. Six more had followed in three away matches versus the New Zealanders and Zimbabwe. But he was not threatening enough for someone being thrown the new ball.

Tactically, we used to look at the first five overs of each

bowler and, if it was the case that they were hanging the ball too wide outside off stump, encourage them to make the batsmen play more. You don't want openers able to leave too many when the ball is at its newest because that is when it's most likely to misbehave.

'Al, you've got to adjust your line closer to off stump.'

'Someone's got to hide it,' he hit back. 'They're going at six an over at the other end!'

Everybody loved him. He was always a magnet for fun and mischief. Take that tour of New Zealand, for example, when in Napier he went out fishing, caught a 5ft shark, lumped it over his shoulder and marched off with it as a souvenir and then went and placed it in Michael Atherton's bed. Or Michael Atherton, England captain, to give him his full title.

In team meetings, everybody would be invited to have a little dig. You don't just want one voice all the time. Players get bored of listening to the captain or coach daily, and someone like Darren Gough, for example, was excellent, although his interjections tended to be 'I will get him out' whenever we analysed an opposition batsman. It didn't matter who it was, Goughie would have them in his sights. Dean Headley would provide a monologue as to what was going to happen, sounding like Barry from *Auf Wiedersehen, Pet*.

The spinners like Robert Croft and Phil Tufnell would provide some input, and then you would finish up with the quieter ones like Graham Thorpe, who wouldn't have said much. Mullally was in the same category as Thorpe.

So, when pushed, what were his pearls of wisdom? Well,

they amounted to: 'Win the toss, rack 'em up, bowl 'em out, bosh, bosh, get your jacket on, go home.' That was Big Al-Mullall for you. Of course, he played for England after qualifying with a British passport but I have to say that he was the most un-Australian Australian I've ever met.

The easy come, easy go nature was reflected in his cricket, too, and his batting was not something he appeared to take too seriously. Of course, when he made it to England level this was a problem and so I told him he would have to knuckle down.

'On occasion, we will need you to get thirty for us. So I need you to stay in and play a bit.'

It was the final of three Tests versus Pakistan in the 1996 home series and, after making scores of 0, 6 and 9* in his three previous innings against them, he walked out to replace centurion John Crawley. With Robert Croft as his partner, he raced to 24 against the genius duo of Waqar Younis and Wasim Akram.

It prompted a shout from the middle to the dressing-room balcony: 'Coach, get 'em in!'

Wherever we went as a team home or abroad, because of his heritage Mullally would seek out the local Irish bar. He was a sucker for Guinness and I had promised him 30 pints of the black stuff if he ever got that score of 30.

Unfortunately, Wasim castled him soon afterwards and that was the end of that.

Phil Tufnell was more of a number 11 and used to argue that batting in net practice too often was counter-productive as it only sapped the confidence further. Trouble was Tuffers played quite regularly with Devon Malcolm, another genuine Jack, and that meant they had to toss a coin for which one was going in for their medicine first. Fifteen times in his 42 Test appearances, Tuffers went in with eight wickets down. With an average of just over five – remember in considering this statistic that number 11s are often left not out as the man at the other end throws caution to the wind – he had opposition attacks licking their lips.

In fact, if you were playing against somebody fast like Courtney Walsh and Curtly Ambrose, the fearsome West Indies duo, he would be asking every couple of minutes in the build-up to the toss: 'What we doing? What we doing? What we doing?'

If we were batting first, he never stopped fretting: 'Oh, Christ, he will kill me. Kill me, I tell you. Can we declare before I get in?'

His type of cricketer doesn't really exist any more. He would get caught at gully or slip – it was no mean feat to nick it behind, considering he would be stood by the square-leg umpire – and he would come off and insist: 'I got into line, I was doing my best.'

It was part of the Tufnell package. He had this reputation for being high maintenance but I flipping loved him. I thought he was brilliant, Athers as captain thought the world of him, and although he would get up to all sorts of scrapes, turning up on a morning dishevelled, like death warmed up, you wouldn't ask.

Equally, we worked out very quickly that when it came to practice with Philip, if you told him 'you bowl in that net', in the expectation of him bowling for a couple of hours, he wouldn't. It would be a response of 'nah, nah, nah'.

But if you reverse things and asked him: 'What do you want to do?' he would come back with: 'All right. I will have a bowl for forty minutes.' And he would end up bowling as long as everyone else. Generally, he knew how much he needed to bowl, didn't like over-bowling and was absolutely fine. Then you could tell him to join in with a few fielding drills, and there would be no trouble with him whatsoever.

Ray Illingworth, the England manager and chairman of selectors prior to my arrival as head coach, said: 'Christ, don't touch him with a barge pole.'

But I always felt with Philip that you needed to cut him some slack. He was a player with a sharp cricket brain, as you hear now on BBC's *Test Match Special,* and always one step ahead of a batsman as a spin bowler. He could play the fool, no doubt. Play it brilliantly. Yet when it came down to it, he knew what he was doing.

It was the changes of pace he was able to feature in his bowling that made him such a threat. And if it was spinning, he was a real handful. Find him the right conditions and he was unplayable. As he proved with 11-wicket match hauls against New Zealand in Christchurch in 1992 and against Australia in the final Ashes Test of 1997 at The Oval.

He seemed to doubt his ability at times, which might have been a bit of a safety net, a bit of an act because he knew what he was doing when it came to the art of slow left-arm. You had to be an accomplished bowler to survive in an era of some seriously good players of spin.

His fielding left something to be desired, though, as proved by his part in what was arguably the worst missed run-out of all time until Nathan Lyon lumbered into Leeds in 2019. It came during a one-day international in Sydney on England's 1990–91 tour of Australia. The Australians were 88 for four batting first with the Waugh twins at the crease when Mark used the depth of the crease to rock back and cut straight to point. With his weight on the back foot, the on-strike batsman wasn't going anywhere and so Steve's injudicious bolt for a single left him at the same end as his sibling as Eddie Hemmings gathered cleanly and lobbed to the bowler's end.

The reaction of my old mate Tony Greig on television commentary to Tufnell's part in the fiasco summed things up. 'Oh my goodness gracious me, you would not believe that was possible,' Greig boomed. Somehow Tuffers managed to drop the lobbed throw. Even then, Waugh's chances of getting back were slim. Only for a bodged shy from four yards by the embarrassed bowler to allow an amble into his ground. The face of England captain Graham Gooch was an absolute picture.

Fitness wasn't his strong point, either, so he had to be cajoled into that, and he was never far away from his beloved cigarettes – even on England duty. On the 1996–97 tour of New Zealand, the ball had been struck out of the nets and it ended up on some spare land adjacent to where the practice was taking place.

Usually in such a scenario somebody goes and fetches it for you, be it one of the backroom team, a net bowler, a fan watching, but on this occasion Tuffers shouted: 'I'll get it.'

'That's odd,' I thought.

But I realised what he was up to when he detoured via his cricket bag. He was after his cigs and lighter. Then, instead of searching for said ball, he positioned himself behind a wall, and therefore out of sight of the rest of us, had a smoke.

On that same theme, we were in Jamaica on a tour of West Indies. To set the scene, it was a training day, and the fitness coach Dean Riddle had said that we were going to leave the Pegasus Hotel and run along the beach wall – one and a half miles out, one and a half miles back.

So I said to Tuffers: 'Right, you can run with me. We will run at the back. But to be clear, we're running, not walking.'

'All right, boss.'

He used to call me 'boss' all the time, like I was a football manager.

'Just hang on a minute. I'll get my fags.'

I could hear his matches rattling in his pocket as we ran, but ran all the way he did and when we got back to base, he was on his hands and knees, sweating like an Alsatian, coughing and wheezing.

'How do you feel, Tuffers?'

'Well, boss,' he said. 'If they ever find anybody that can hit it three miles, I'll be able to fetch it back!'

As a young player with Middlesex, he had a few moments of ill discipline, and would get up to all sorts, legal or illegal, but other than being a bit of a Jack the Lad, there was no harm in him at all. He has a very likeable personality, as we saw when he was crowned king of the jungle in *I'm A Celebrity . . . Get Me Out Of Here!*, and made it beyond half-way in *Strictly Come Dancing*.

He has gained a popularity outside cricket as a mainstream TV face, popping up on BBC Television's *The One Show* and *A Question of Sport* regularly and, like Flintoff, his character has really come out as a broadcaster.

CHAPTER 11

The Modern Game

Kevin Pietersen is quite simply the best batsman I have seen play for England. Yes, he joined a team on the rise. Under Michael Vaughan's leadership they were unbeaten in Test cricket throughout 2004, completed an historic series win in the Caribbean and strung together eight consecutive victories. He took them to the next level.

Let me level something with you here. I don't know Kevin. What I mean by that is he is not someone I have become friendly with. Of course, we have had chats, lots of 'good mornings' as we have gone about our respective day's work, but nothing has developed beyond that professional relationship. The long-distance relationship we have had from the middle to the commentary box, however, has been a rewarding one from my perspective.

As someone who has played for, prepared and critiqued the national team over four decades, I have not seen anyone on his level in an England shirt. He demanded all eyes were on him with the way he performed. What a presence at the crease he possessed. He was commanding from the moment he arrived and had that knack of shoving a fielding team from the front foot onto the back.

There were so many memorable innings during a top-level career that ran from late 2004 to early 2014, and one that should have spanned much longer. There was the double hundred in Adelaide during the 2010–11 Ashes, the 151 in the heat of Colombo versus Sri Lanka in 2012 and the series-changing 186 in Mumbai later in that year. However, the innings I would have to select as the most influential was the 158 at The Oval in 2005 because, for all the brilliance of Andrew Flintoff and that fabulous bowling attack that came before it that summer, without it England arguably wouldn't have reclaimed those Ashes.

It was just audacious brilliance and his duel with Shane Warne was captivating. The shots he was playing against the spin over midwicket made you think, watching on, 'He's going to sky one, here'. That was what Shane Warne must have thought, too. But KP didn't sky one. He just kept hitting the ball in the middle of the bat, and with every strike he put England further out of Australia's reach.

His attacking instincts were what made him stand out for me. No one had ever plonked Glenn McGrath into the Lord's pavilion during a Test match until that summer. He showed his teammates that there was a happy medium between careful and carefree.

We had that sort of player in the 1970s in Clive Lloyd – someone who dragged everybody else along. We were

English and defensive batsmen by default. We would get behind the ball – 'Nothing's getting past this lot' – as a first instinct. Then this loose-limbed West Indian comes along and goes bang, bang, bang. Witnessing a teammate doing that makes you think about your own game, the limitations you are setting upon yourself, and encourages you to bring a little bit more adventure into things. He gave us the encouragement to be more expansive.

Pietersen always played the situation but his priority was to get on with it and push the scoreboard and his physical attributes were key to this – being very tall for a batsman, he possessed a massive stride when playing on the front foot and his long levers allowed him to get right out to the ball. For a big man he was also very agile. Surprisingly so. That ability to get down the pitch quickly, allied to very fast hands, made him so dangerous against spin.

He also held an unbelievable level of confidence. Off the scale, really. In his head I imagine he was always telling himself, no matter who he was up against: 'This bloke can't bowl to me.' England were glad of any superiority complex when he was out in the middle and he worked unbelievably hard, as all the very best batsmen do, on his own game. It was unorthodox but he had it honed to perfection. He saw the ball early and his gigantic reach allowed him to access it and hit it from well in front of his body. This allowed him to generate immense power.

In stature he reminded me of Ted Dexter. Ted was also a real swashbuckler in the 1960s. Lord Ted, as he was known, liked to give it a tap.

Looking from the outside in, Pietersen was successful by being the one who bucked the trend. He challenged convention. If someone told him to do it one way, he would do it a different way. As if to prove he could do it both ways, but the better way was his way. What made him such a good player was that he was able to work out what was the right method and approach for him. In an international team, you cannot regiment everyone. You need some individuality and that was what he was all about. It was evident that he was resistant to working with Graham Gooch, who was the England batting consultant for a time. He would go and seek out his trusted adviser in Graham Ford, someone he first knew from his time as a young player in South Africa.

I have always advocated players consulting their go-to men for technical advice. If you want to work with your own man then that is fine. When you get to that level, you know what works for you and what doesn't and the key is to make sure you are as prepared as you can be to keep up the standards required for international cricket. An example from my time as England coach is Darren Gough, who would always insist on communicating ideas to, and looked for advice from, Steve Oldham. When you have risen through the ranks as a player at a particular county and been successful, it stands to reason that you would want to confide in those who helped you get there. Not least because they are the ones that know your game best. We would have bowling coaches on hand should he want to use them, but I respected that he trusted his own man at Yorkshire.

From day one we knew that Kevin was his own man and

the ruthless way in which he navigated his pathway to the England team spoke of his determination. It takes some cojones to leave South Africa in the manner that he did and turn up in England looking for a county.

That was quite a drastic measure to take in my view, but he was a young player who knew where he was going. He was also in quite a hurry to get there. Nottinghamshire benefited from his ambition, picking him up after he had been on trial at Warwickshire, and it is fair to say that he left a mark on them and everywhere he went throughout his career.

My observations from a distance are that he was a complex character and only became more complex because of everything that had been said and written about him. Overall, I thought his treatment by England was poor, that he should never have been sacked.

Let me expand. If you have a problem with a player, deal with it. If said player steps out of line, bring him back into line. Suspend him if you like, make him kick his heels without playing for a while, but ride the storm and be honest. They should have been explicit in listing his particular misdemeanours at the end of the 2013–14 tour of Australia, not left it to conjecture.

It also intrigued me how much he divided opinion among his teammates. It was really polarised across the dressing room. Some said he was great, some said he was not, but whatever anyone within the team thought of him, one thing could not be disputed – he would win you cricket matches. And that is why I would have disciplined him instead of ditching him.

Yes, Pietersen's problems habitually appeared to stem from the breakdown of his relationship with his own teammates, which is staggering. We've all played in teams where we haven't got on with a particular player, and you just have to work through it. Anyone who thinks all teams are harmonious hasn't played in teams much.

I will give you an example which, although light-hearted in essence, provides an example of this. It came during a talk I was asked to give to the Lancashire squad over the winter of 2019–20. I had been asked along to Westhoughton Cricket Club by Paul Allott, the director of cricket, and Glen Chapple, the first-team coach, to address the players.

I talked about various subjects on county cricket culture and on the subject of team spirit I reminded them of the need for tolerance. The fact that there would be players of difference. The fact that there is a shit in every dressing room. It was a serious reflection, provided with some levity afterwards when Alex Davies, the club's England Lions wicketkeeper-batsman, sidled up to me and declared: 'I am that shit!'

Of course, the KP breakdown was more serious than being a constant pain in the arse. With him it appeared to have been a complete breakdown in trust with other senior players. He was quite a sensitive soul and did not react well to what he perceived to be his teammates taking a rise out of him. Any involvement with the KP Genius Twitter account from inside the dressing room was denied. But he was clearly very upset. Again, it should have been sorted out.

Dressing rooms can be unforgiving places but it is a domain for everyone to come together for the common good, and if everyone is not coming together, it is the responsibility of all within that team to sort out the problems. Do not for one minute assume that even those dressing rooms of the most successful teams in history are all hunky-dory. They are not. Flash points occur. But they blow over and things settle down over time.

I would have expected senior players to have dealt with those incidents involving Pietersen better than they did. Junior players would have no influence. But there were enough players of standing to have realised that they were all behaving like kids and for the betterment of the England team it should have been sorted out. You don't have to like the bloke who is sat next to you, but one thing should be mutual if you are an international teammate and that is respect. You don't have to have things in common to be able to work alongside someone and do a job.

A number of people were clearly hurt by Pietersen, so I am not suggesting the fault is totally on the other side. I cannot judge what went on because, like you, I was not party to internal events. But what we do know is that he fell out big time with a core of four very established figures in that England team of the time in Andrew Strauss, Alastair Cook, Matt Prior and Graeme Swann. It's sad it came to that and they couldn't accommodate one of our greatest players.

Kevin also had a huge clash of personalities with Peter Moores, someone I always found to be a decent bloke. There was a total lack of communication between the pair and it was clear from what he said subsequently that Pietersen, as captain, did not rate Moores as a coach. Players do not select coaches, administrators do, and it is a player's responsibility to work alongside the appointed man as effectively as possible. Not liking someone's style is something you should be able to work through. That breakdown, which led to Moores' removal as coach in early 2009, was also handled badly.

The bottom line is that England lost a great player. Pietersen would still have been hugely influential for two to three years when they cut him.

As a batsman, he thrived when there was any sort of conflict. Recall his first major tour in the winter of 2004–05 when the crowds in his native South Africa booed him incessantly and turned their backs on him – until the final match when they kept facing the front and showered him in applause. I would argue that he had to be riled to play at his best – by either his own team or his opposition. Studying him fascinates me because his character was complex and analysing him tells you something of what makes a great player.

But I admired the way that he batted because he fitted perfectly into a no-fear edict. The England team had spent decades being careful and he transformed the style in which the team could play. You have to remember that the selectors sacrificed Graham Thorpe, a veteran of 100 Tests and a batsman with a fine international record, to accommodate him. It was undoubtedly because Michael Vaughan saw such a change would make England a more progressive team.

Vaughan got the best out of him and I can't help but think that, had he been able to continue as England captain rather than succumb to a succession of knee injuries, everything might have been handled very differently. For whatever reason, first Paul Downton, and then Andrew Strauss, Downton's successor in the director of cricket role, could not find a way to prolong Pietersen's England days.

Cricket supporters are influenced by great cricketers and through his performances Pietersen won many people over. What a shame he couldn't win over his own team. Frank Sinatra's song 'My Way' suited him perfectly. The bottom line is that he should have been playing for England in the manner he did from the moment Vaughan told him to go out and be himself at lunch on day five at The Oval in September 2005. He did so, he didn't change for the next few years and England benefited massively. I cannot recall anyone in the game attracting as much interest as this particular lad. He was different and he was special.

That is also a term that can be used for Jimmy Anderson. There might be a greater debate to be had as to whether he is England's best ever bowler, but in terms of volume of wickets and consistency of performance over a period of time, there can be no argument. No other seamer in the history of the game has taken as many Test wickets.

It gives me a sense of pride that Anderson is from my county, Lancashire. A lot of bowlers use grumpiness as self-motivation, and he is one of them. Nothing is ever good enough. It ensures he keeps his own bar high. Glenn McGrath was very similar when it came to the standards he set and his reaction to any hint of a drop. They are both quiet, really nice blokes until you put cricket whites on them. Glenn would think nothing of chuntering at himself and swearing on his way back to third man. At times, when the red mist descends, it looks pretty obvious to me that Jim hates batsmen.

It has been an extraordinary journey from those early days when Bob Willis used the Sky Sports lazy switch to let out his expletive at the pace he was witnessing, and one that had the most testing of starts. At the end of his very first full county season, Jimmy was sent to England's academy in Adelaide under the guidance of its director Rodney Marsh.

It was there that Marsh said, 'Jimmy has a lot of work to do on his action.' The advice from the bowling experts was that he needed to revamp it otherwise he'd only last five years. And they tried to remodel it working with the bowling coach Troy Cooley. Jimmy debuted for England that winter of 2002–03 and while he was doing just fine on the field, he was at the drawing board off it.

This went on for some time before Jimmy eventually said: 'No, I'm going back to what I know.' In that regard, Jimmy was Troy Cooley's one failure. Cooley was lauded for the influence he had over the 2005 Ashes attack, but this course of action coincided with Anderson almost being broken. Of course, the ECB coaching team were only acting for the best and, in his youth, Jimmy charged into the crease, then dipped his head right down into the off-side in delivering the ball, landing over a splayed front leg. There has been a slight modification of all this rather than a complete overhaul and it has served him well.

The lad with the skunk on the top of his head and a mullet at the back started off as Banksy and he's finished up as Rembrandt. These days, when he gets into his delivery stride, he just checks momentarily – there's a definite check before he releases the ball. It's the moment that he sets his body and that gives him extra control. Whereas previously he would just run in and let it go, there is a more measured finish now that can actually be seen across his full run-up. Every now and again you will see him pull up after just a couple of yards and return to the start, which is a sign that he has lost his stride pattern into the crease. Equally, look at the economy of movement. His last five strides before the release of the ball are really explosive. That's a bowler who knows his game inside out.

It might only have been against Zimbabwe but his first five-wicket haul for England, on his Test debut at Lord's in 2003, made you sit up. Nasser Hussain, then England captain, used to enthuse about what he offered the team with the new ball. 'He swings it but he swings it late,' Hussain would say.

As with any swing bowler, if it goes from the hand it is nowhere near as dangerous as when the ball moves on the latter half of its journey. A young Anderson did not always get it right but when he did, it was dynamite because when the ball swings at a speed close to 90 mph, a batsman who plays down the wrong line has no time to adjust. When the ball swings from the hand you have 18 yards for your eyes to pick up its path but if it swings in its last third of travel, you've got a problem.

Being able to swing the ball like that is a God-given talent. Before this, I hadn't realised God had dished out any gifts in Burnley. It is not one that has been lost. In the first Test match of 2020, Anderson came back from the best part of six months off due to injury, bowled like he'd never been away and took yet another Test five-for in match figures of 37-15-63-7, to set up a series-levelling victory against South Africa in Cape Town.

There has been so much talk about his powers waning, particularly overseas, yet his performances in his 37th and 38th years made a mockery of such suggestions. He took wickets, and was the best bowler on show, in both the Test match versus West Indies in Barbados and that Newlands fixture 12 months apart. Throughout his later career I have become sick of comments about Jimmy not being able to do this, not been able to do that. My staple reply tends to be, 'Well, there's a lot of things he can do.'

That was my attitude during my time as a coach. Others might focus on weaknesses but all I wanted a player to think about was what they were good at. Things in need of improvement can be worked upon but I wanted them to think positively about their best skills.

It has been noticeable that his pace doesn't change year on year either. Since he became an established new-ball international bowler in 2008 there has been no obvious drop-off. He is bowling at exactly the same pace now as he was a decade ago and isn't taking anything out of himself to do so. I can still see him bowling for England at 40. Age is just a number to him and there is nothing to say he won't be performing exactly the same as he is now.

I do not anticipate him doing so at 75 mph either. He is still at 83–84 and although he's had a couple of wear and tear injuries he's still as fit as a fiddle and very ambitious. Drive and ambition are very important to retain. I hope he has not missed out financially from it but from a cricketing perspective it was a good thing that he was withdrawn from one-day cricket by England in the build-up to the 2015 World Cup. We don't want to see a bowler of his ilk carted all over the show and it has narrowed his focus. Give him a red ball. See how he does with that. Generally, he puts it into danger areas for batsmen in the most relentless fashion.

Some of the great bowlers of my era operated in a similar way as their career deepened. Malcolm Marshall, Andy Roberts and Richard Hadlee all showed you didn't have to be rapid quick, just be highly skilled with the ball. The subtlety is in the ability to change the pace slightly. Hadlee bowled with unerring accuracy, and in his bowling plan he would bowl at, say, 80 per cent capacity. Then every now and again he would shift it up to 100. The effect? The batsman would then be wondering: woah, where has that come from? It's similar to golf. A top golfer would only swing at 80 per cent, doesn't give it full whack until it is absolutely necessary.

Cricket supporters in this country will only know how good Anderson and his long-term new-ball partner, Stuart Broad, are when they're not there. That's when their true worth will show.

This dastardly duo are England's best-ever opening partnership. It's there in the stats, staring you in the face. In the last decade, they were number one and two in the leading wicket-takers' list in Tests: Anderson with 429 at an average of 24.35; Broad 403 at 27.65. Of their nearest rivals, only the spin trio of Nathan Lyon, Rangana Herath and Ravichandran Ashwin got more than 267.

When you go through the high-class opening partnerships that England have had since the Second World War, there has been Brian Statham and Fred Trueman, Bob Willis and Ian Botham, Darren Gough and Andy Caddick, and Steve Harmison and Matthew Hoggard. All were absolutely terrific. Anderson and Broad are tops.

They have shown great leadership in the way they have looked after themselves, setting the standards for others to follow, and it's very apparent that they help each other. These two are always talking to each other and to other bowlers. Not only on the field but in practice, sharing knowledge. That has not always been the case with top players. Some keep it to themselves whereas these two pass it on quite freely.

What I admire about Broad is that he has never rested on his laurels. I've never seen him walk out onto a field with an England shirt on and not put in. He's trying like billy-o all the time. Partly that is down to personal pride; partly it has been the competition for places for national team selection at times. He can be quite bloody-minded and when he sees a threat develop on the horizon, a possibility that somebody might take his place, he develops an over-my-dead-body attitude.

Whenever Broad comes under pressure for his place, he comes up with new tricks. He changed his run-up and delivery stride during the winter of 2018–19 when he was left out against Sri Lanka and it had impressive effects. Similarly, the previous year he had worked out for himself that he was letting his fingers slip down the side of the ball, rather than holding them proud over the seam.

Broad might have an angelic face but he's got a mean streak. He's a very combative cricketer and someone who likes to be involved in rucks with opponents. Think of the time he nicked one to slip and stood his ground in the 2013 Ashes. The uproar in Australia was incredible. What a reaction – from Australians, of all people!

Suddenly, they were a nation who believed in walking. Darren Lehmann, the Australia coach, urged the public down under to send him home crying for the second of back-to-back series that year. Well, I can tell you that Broad will have loved the entire conflict. He loves a scrap.

As a bowler he tends to get on hot streaks during which he looks like he might bowl teams out on his own. You can certainly tell when Broad gets excited that conditions and his performance have aligned perfectly. At this point he really pumps into the crease with his legs.

It's not that he doesn't fancy it at other times; it's just that something clicks when it's his day. He recognises when it's his moment and he sees those moments more often than not against Australia. Think of The Oval and his inspired spell in 2009 or the eight wickets he bagged at Trent Bridge in 2015. And he quite likes conditions in South Africa, too. His performance at the Wanderers in 2016 was something else.

Sadly, his batting has gone since August 2014 when the India fast bowler Varun Aaron struck him a blow in the face with a bouncer. It placed a mental hurdle he has, as yet, been unable to get over, and it has been a bugbear of mine that within this machine that is Team England we haven't had the personnel to put things right.

The ECB employs psychologists in addition to coaches to work with England teams and yet they have not been able to get Broad over his fear of the ball, thus denying him the chance to get anywhere near the quality of batting he'd previously shown, averaging in excess of 30 over his first 20 Test matches, and scoring a career-best 169 versus Pakistan at Lord's in his 32nd back in 2011. That average has since plunged into the teens and there should be people within that group who are able to address the decline, put it right and tap back into that natural ability; he's regressed to the point where it is beyond debate that he is a number 10 or 11.

But as a bowler, along with Anderson, there has been no such dip in standards. We will miss them when they are gone. Just as we have missed that great entertainer Pietersen.

CHAPTER 12

The Ben

The English game has been lucky to have had a few players who can be referred to as the complete cricketer. To that list add the name of Ben Stokes.

It is not a title to be dished out lightly and for me the baton has passed from Ian Botham to Andrew Flintoff and on to Stokes, after a truly outstanding 18 months in an England shirt. He is as good as either of his two predecessors, both of whom have famously slain Australia in epic home series. I would never resort to saying, 'He's better than him and he's better than him,' because putting them on a level footing is praise enough.

It is always hard to compare era to era anyway, Botham being in his pomp 40 years ago and Flintoff 15, but there are shared traits running through this trio of English all-rounders.

Beefy's stats stack up over a period of time, especially when he was fully functional from a physical perspective. Things were different later in his international career when his back had gone but ponder this: he had been so good, had created such a presence on the field that he could con opponents into thinking he still had it.

My feeling on Flintoff has always been the same: if you wanted something to happen on a cricket field, if the game was at its tipping point, he was the man to turn to. Michael Vaughan knew this only too well and, by the height of summer in 2005, the entire country knew it, too.

What we saw during the calendar year of 2019 was Stokes carrying the mantle brilliantly, replicating both of these potentially match-winning qualities. Like Botham, opponents began to do unusual things against him, lose their discipline in decisive moments, and like Flintoff he mastered the art of seizing the moment. When it was needed most, the mix of aura and audacity would come out.

The game of cricket needs superstars and he is right up there. The fact that he was named as BBC Sports Personality of the Year in 2019 after his performances during the World Cup and Ashes was only a good thing for the sport. That public vote was an acceptance that this bloke's as good as we've got in any chosen field.

The thing about that particular award is that personality is the key word. His personality shines through. He's got great charisma. And he is a leader. When they took his vice-captaincy off him because of previous off-field events it didn't take him long to go back and say to the ECB chief executive Tom Harrison: I'm vice-captain, and I want my job back. He felt compelled to do it and that's proper leadership.

Yes, it is undeniable that Stokes made a couple of wrong turnings, but people make mistakes in life; name me somebody that hasn't. My view on the Bristol incident is that the suspensions and the court case that followed have definitely driven him on and he's come out of it a better lad and a miles better player.

He's always had this fiery temperament and that's not going to change. He's edgy. You should hear how he blames me for letting positions go when we are partners at golf. If he starts throwing his clubs, as is his wont, I goad him with: 'Is that the furthest you can fling 'em?'

And so I chuckled when he had that verbal altercation with the bloke in the crowd at the Wanderers, on the 2019–20 tour of South Africa, after he had been called a fat ginger Ed Sheeran as he was about to enter the ground's distinctive tunnel to the dressing room.

The response of 'Come out the back and say that, you four-eyed c***' was proper Ben.

When I got out there for the one-day internationals we met up a couple of times on the outfield before play. 'Have you found that four-eyed c*** yet?' I asked him.

'Don't you start!' he told me.

I know he was reprimanded by the match officials, in the form of a 15 per cent match-fee fine, but I didn't see any malice in the incident at all. I considered it hilarious and had tears in my eyes when I heard newsreaders referencing the exchange back in the UK. Tell me how else someone subjected to a fan running over to deliver such abuse immediately after their dismissal was going to react. Rory Burns had said the same thing to someone who offered some post-dismissal advice in the Old Trafford Ashes Test five months earlier. And I reckon that geezer would have been absolutely thrilled. He would have been bragging to all his mates down the pub: 'Guess what he called me?'

What Stokes did with the bat during the 2019 summer was Bothamesque. Twice England found themselves in positions where the game was gone. First at Lord's in the World Cup final and then in the Ashes Test match at Headingley when he found himself with only Jack Leach left for company.

It coincided with a greater maturity to his cricket. He'll now play the situation perfectly. He's got a great technique, a rock-solid defence, but has opposition teams on edge because he can switch gears whenever he wants and he knows when to change gear. Knowledge is everything in this regard. He has shown an aptitude for waiting for somebody to stay with him, get a partnership going and then off they go.

The fact that he has that patience makes other teams wary of him. Generally speaking, his technique means they have got to get him out. There's no obvious weakness. And he's all power. People suggest that this is down to the size of the bats. Not really. It's the power of the player. Of course, you want good equipment, and all sports equipment is getting better, but you put any decent bat in his hands and he can be devastating.

What an example he gave in playing the long game in the World Cup final against New Zealand when he got into that bubble of his, alongside Jos Buttler, to steady the chase of 242, and then exploded into life at the back end. Granted, there were moments of fortune: Trent Boult standing on the rope at long on to add six to the England total, and that barely believable deflection off Stokes's bat face when diving to make his ground contributing to six more. But he remained blinkered to the pressure until the very end, then repeated it in the super over.

In Headingley's modern miracle, his best attributes were to the fore in undiluted form. To negotiate such a long period of the game on the third evening and score two off 50 balls takes some discipline for a front-line batsman. But he has spoken about visualising the type of innings he wants to play during his assessment of bowlers and conditions on the dressing-room balcony before walking out to bat, and he had already conceived the plan to be not out at the close come what may. In terms of execution, it proved as effective as any of his extraordinary strokes the following day.

On that fourth morning, he knew that he had the ability to change gear when required. Very few can do that. Very few. And it is what has separated the world-class players all through the ages. The likes of Viv Richards, Ricky Ponting and Kevin Pietersen could all up tempo, but I don't think I have ever seen such a dramatic change in a batsman's scoring rate in Test cricket. During that fabulous unbeaten 135, it went from three in his first 66 deliveries to 165 across his final 48.

The cricket itself was a real throwback to what Botham did during his 149 not out against Dennis Lillee and company in 1981. Australian bowling attacks old and new rendered powerless. We are talking about some brilliant bowlers in Pat Cummins, Josh Hazlewood, James Pattinson and Nathan Lyon and some cases Stokes was hitting them 10 rows back.

The self-belief in pulling off this heist was incredible and it was fascinating to observe him talking Jack Leach through what he wanted to do from 73 required to win with one wicket left standing. Within a quarter of an hour or so Australia had just gone. Absolutely gone.

They weren't winning that match from a relatively long way out despite the dominant position they had been in previously. With 17 required, Marcus Harris put down a sprawling chance running in from third man, then came the ridiculous review for lbw when a Pat Cummins delivery was so obviously pitched outside Leach's leg stump. And when Nathan Lyon dropped the ball in what would have been the run-out of Jack Leach and a one-run Australian win, people lacked sympathy because of his previous behaviour, such as dropping the ball on A. B. de Villiers when he did enact a run-out in Durban the previous year.

The latter two were barely believable happenings but thankfully for the contest – and this isn't me speaking as someone with an England shirt on – they did happen because otherwise Australia's review against Stokes on the next ball after the run-out bodge-up would have resulted in a highly controversial finish.

To this day I say 'not out', no matter what Hawkeye says to the contrary. The projection of the ball's trajectory just didn't look right when it was shown to be hitting the stumps. It was heading down leg-side and yet the graphic somehow had it straightening, not after pitching, but on contact with Stokes's pad. The line Hawkeye predicted just looked wrong and I fully understand, having been an umpire myself, why Joel Wilson didn't give it out. You have got to be certain it is out to give a leg before and he clearly couldn't be. Australian fingers after the match should not have been pointing accusingly at others but at their own team after they lost the opportunity to review. Just stupid.

Australian minds were scrambled, though, because Stokes had taken on their world-class bowlers and reduced them to nonentities by blasting the ball to all parts.

It was an incredible execution of a game plan under pressure, after recognising from his vantage point as a not-out batsman in the dressing room that the only way England could win was for him to be there unbeaten at the start of day four. It was proved to be a superb evaluation.

Stokes is an extremely hardy character. On the field he might look indestructible at times but he has come through a lot. Like the devastating experience in the final of the World Twenty20 in 2016, when he felt like his world had collapsed at the hands of Carlos Brathwaite's hitting. As I say, he came out of the Bristol fracas a better person and when his dad Ged was seriously ill in South Africa in 2019–20, he played on and got through it.

That would have been tough because Stokes is a family man at heart, and his own son Layton is a real chip off the old block. During the previous tour of South Africa in 2015–16, there was a barbecue night organised at the villas where a number of the players were staying. The pram, pushed by

Ben's wife, Clare, stopped and out jumped this toddler. Two steps and he leapt straight into the swimming pool, fully clothed. It was pretty obvious whose kid it was!

Everybody will recognise the tough-guy traits in that action but the toughness I like most in Stokes is his response to pain. All cricketers play with niggles, but he plays through them. Some players are very fragile and at the least bit of a twinge the answer is 'no'. Not him: he just goes through it, whether it be pain in his knees, his toes, his back. He knows you're not going to be bang on all the time, but that you've just got to get through.

A good example of this was earlier in his heroic Headingley display when he was bowling through a bit of discomfort and ended up sending down 15 overs in a row from one end. England regularly publicise the fact that they are trying to manage his workload by limiting his bowling but whenever they broach that subject, I always wonder: have you told Ben that?

Or considered the fact that he can be as effective as a front-line bowler in all kinds of varying conditions? Whether it be running in and pounding the pitch in unresponsive conditions like this instance or when lateral movement is prodigious. He can be like Roy of the Rovers at times. Think back to his six-wicket haul at Trent Bridge which helped seal the 2015 Ashes when he was bending it like Beckham. Or to the swing he was producing at good pace against West Indies in another match that decided a series in 2017, against West Indies at Lord's, when he took six for 22 and left Jimmy Anderson waiting for his big moment on 499 wickets.

In theory it's a sound notion to reduce his input on the bowling side of his all-rounder status but have you tried getting the ball out of his hand? He would think it was an affront if you took him off after five overs. He would want eight, nine or ten.. That's a spell of bowling to him and he gives it everything. Absolutely everything.

And he starts ticking when he doesn't get it right. Don't get me wrong, I love his attitude, his commitment and ability, but I cannot suppress the giggles if he slides one down the leg-side and it gets whacked for four. You can put money on what follows. There will be a kick of a sod beneath his feet, a bit like Angus Fraser used to do back in the 1990s.

But this kind of reaction, like his histrionics after poor strokes on the golf course, shows how deeply committed he is. He is the first name on any team sheet, and those are the kind of characters around whom you build a team.

While Stokes has undoubtedly found himself as a cricketer, it is fair to say that despite sustained personal and team success Jos Buttler has not. Now the thing that makes Jos Buttler stand out is his versatility. You would tend to think of him as a modern-day power player, a game changer, but because he has so much going for him as a batsman I am not sure, even as he nears 30, what his best position or role within the team is in limited-overs cricket. Whether it's as a finisher, in the middle of an innings or opening and blazing away at the start.

What I would say is that this is the lesser of his issues because he has been successful in each of the roles. His more pressing issue is why − as a player with all the shots, and a seemingly perfect temperament – has he not cracked Test cricket? Why is he still waiting to happen as a Test batsman? Mark my words, there is a Test player there, most definitely.

Partly it's because he hasn't got to grips with the position of number seven. It's a very difficult place to bat because Test matches can evolve quickly sometimes and batting at seven means there is every chance that you watch eight, nine, ten and eleven blown away either by a wrist spinner or pace.

Yet the one player who really cracked it in this position was also a wicketkeeper: Adam Gilchrist of Australia. There was not much in terms of batting depth coming behind him either, but he had that knack of farming the strike and playing his shots at the appropriate times. Buttler remains betwixt and between whether he wants to play like a Test player or play like Jos Buttler. Well, play like Jos Buttler would be my advice. Take them on.

Sometimes people forget themselves in first-class cricket. They have so much of their own personality coming through when the ball is white and there is a restriction on the number of deliveries they can possibly face. They tend to respond to those kinds of constraints. Conversely, provide them with ultimate freedom and it's as if they feel they cannot be themselves.

And it happens to the best, as I witnessed during the 2019 domestic summer when I watched Eoin Morgan playing for Middlesex v Lancashire in a County Championship match at Lord's. It was an early season match, played in the first half of April, and Lancashire's Australian import Glenn Maxwell was bowling off-spin. Morgan had got one run off about

20 balls and the field was up. He just kept blocking and
I'm saying to myself 'just play like Eoin Morgan,' as if the
England one-day captain is stood within earshot rather than
150 yards away.

If you had put coloured clothes on him and changed the
ball from red to white, he would have plonked Maxwell
into the stands. Sometimes, there's a mental process that
makes players change: 'Oh, this is a four-day game, this is a
Test match, I've got to play like . . .' So instead of peppering
the nursery end of the ground, Morgan played in a more
restrained manner and got out for single figures.

There is something to be said for playing your way, whatever that might be, as Gilchrist did. The Australians who
played alongside him reckon they constantly told him 'don't
look at the scoreboard'. That it didn't matter how many the
others had got; they wanted him to go and play his way, and
there's a lot to be said for that.

Others would counter with: 'Well, you've got to play
responsibly.' For me, though, you've got to back your skill,
back your judgement and play your way. Every now and again
there will be a failure, there might even be barren periods,
but you've got to look at his value to the team as a potential
changer of a game's course, and reassure him over his place.

There's always debate as to whether it should be Jonny
Bairstow, Jos Buttler or Ben Foakes behind the stumps, but
personally I would be playing Bairstow and Buttler. Jonny
Bairstow's got six Test match hundreds and he's just had a bad
trot. Again, there's a proper Test match player there.

England have had greater clarity on what they want from

Buttler when it comes to Twenty20 cricket, and it first came up while he was with the Indian Premier League. Rajasthan Royals simply decided that the more deliveries he faces the more damage he is going to do and therefore it is best to send him in first.

He doesn't lack power – both Buttler and Ben Stokes are as fit as anyone when it comes to international cricket, possessing what I would call it extreme fitness. They put so much into getting themselves in top physical condition and to my mind there must be something about getting muscly – not muscle-bound – that means they can hit the ball miles.

Yet Buttler optimises the chance to play no-fear cricket with the deft side of batting, too. He can sweep, reverse-sweep and ramp for fun. Even when bowlers are sending the ball down at 80-plus mph. To be able to take on balls at that speed and hit them not only over your own head but the keeper's head, too – that's outrageous and takes a great deal of confidence.

So what of his character? Well, he has a fairly reserved demeanour. But don't be fooled by him. There is another side to him. Yes, he's actually a generally quiet chap on the field but when the England team used to play football as a warm-up, something that the coach Chris Silverwood was forced to outlaw during the winter of 2019–20 when Rory Burns was sidelined following an injury incurred while dodging an attempted Joe Root tackle, Buttler was not so quiet.

Just ask the referees of these matches. Mark Saxby, the team's rubber, or Phil Neale, the operations manager, or yours truly – yes, I've been roped in to officiate a few times – will tell you the same thing. There always seems to be one bloke you have to keep your eye on in these kinds of matches and when I first took the whistle, everybody told me: 'Watch Buttler.'

They weren't flippin' kidding. He's an absolute bloody nightmare. These games are only 10 minutes each way but for the full duration he is incessant. Even when you can't see him, you can hear him. He's always in your ear.

Kevin Pietersen famously dubbed Peter Moores 'the Woodpecker' but that nickname could not be more applicable to Buttler, who is always pecking away with advice like 'You're too slow, referee, get up with play.'

I also saw another ruthlessly competitive side to him when we played golf at Mere in Cheshire. We are part of the same management group along with Joe Root and Ben Stokes and on the annual golf day I tend to play with Ben. Or at least I used to until he got fed up with our partnership and my observations that he's the kind of golfer that goes out with 14 clubs and comes back with 12.

One will get snapped over his knee and another will resemble a tie around a neck on the trunk of a tree.

Golf is a game based on handicaps. If you play at all this is very familiar to you. I play a bit and my handicap is 10. As a member of a golf club, as I am, you tend to know what it is.

Ask Jos what his handicap is, though, and you will be met with silence.

'We will give you a clue, Jos. The answer is a number.'

'I will play off sixteen today.'

'Are you sure? Sixteen? Are you a member of a golf club?'

'No.'

'Well, where do you get sixteen from then?'

'Well, I haven't been playing much recently and so I'll play off sixteen.'

I couldn't help feeling that we were being screwed on this particular subject. Something that seemed to be confirmed when we took on one of the course's par five holes. Jos drives off and lands the ball in the semi-rough, about 250 yards from the pin. He then proceeds to pull a rescue club from his bag and stiffs the ball to within a metre of the flag, walking away with an eagle three in the process. He hits low-draw shots like Waqar Younis used to bowl reverse swing.

'What's your handicap again, Jos?'

In golf parlance, he's a Mexican. He has no shame whatsoever.

On the field, he tends to be quite withdrawn but he will stand up for himself if roused, as was the case with Vernon Philander during England's Test series in South Africa in 2019–20 when he chirped up with 'Get your gut out the way, knobhead,' as Philander's full figure obscured his view of a throw from the infield to the batsman's end.

From what I could gather listening to the stump microphones, the South African had not said a word but something had got Jos going, and he received a 15 per cent match-fee fine for his trouble.

And he has on occasion become a magnet for controversy on the field, too. Recall him being Mankaded by Ravichandran Ashwin in a match between Rajasthan Royals and Kings XI Punjab at the 2019 Indian Premier League.

Buttler had made 69 and was left furious by an incident that altered the course of a game that Punjab went on to win.

Everybody in world cricket has a view on the Mankad issue. The number one rule for me is that a batsman must stay in his ground. But there is a big difference to me in a player trying to steal ground and being absent-minded. We all know that a batsman at the non-striker's end cannot leave his ground until the ball has been delivered but, equally, the bowler cannot feign a delivery, which is what is happening more and more, and, in my opinion, is what happened in this particular situation.

It wasn't as if Buttler was dancing down the pitch and replays suggested he arguably would have been in his ground at the point at which the bowler (Ashwin) would have been expected to deliver, as law 41 states. He just dragged his bat out of its ground in expectation that it would happen.

The grey area here is that any benefit of the doubt goes to the bowler, not the batsman, and so anyone who does not remain in his ground is out. Well, I agree entirely when it is attempting to stop sharp practice. But I do have a problem when it becomes sharp practice in itself. There is a big difference between trying to steal a march and ordinarily backing up. Anyone can pull a dummy and, instead of bowling the ball, take the bails off.

I would wager that it could be done at any stage during a match and you could bet your bottom dollar the batsman would have left his crease. But as happened infamously in West Indies' narrow win over Zimbabwe at the Under-19 World Cup in 2016, a bowler should not be able to contrive this scenario. There must be a way of ensuring the individual in question has in some part got into the mechanical motion of the bowling action before they can do it to make the delivery active. On that occasion, Keemo Paul did not get into any kind of delivery stride.

As with the picture I have painted of him so far, Buttler is a steelier character than he is given credit for. He may play in a carefree manner, but he cares deeply and I have no doubt that this episode and Ashwin's involvement in it will be stored in the memory banks.

Buttler has history, too. I cannot think of many others who have been dismissed in this manner twice. Think back to England's one-day international against Sri Lanka at Edgbaston in 2014 when Sachithra Senanayake took the bails off. On that occasion, I got into an exchange of opinion on social media with the former *Guardian* cricket correspondent Mike Selvey, who was right when he said, 'It's not hard to stay in your ground.' The Sri Lankans had warned him twice in the 42nd over and undoubtedly felt it was not breaking the spirit of the game to uphold his exit in the 44th. Nor is it hard to run up to the crease with no intention of delivering the ball.

Players like Buttler didn't exist in my playing or coaching days. Crikey, no. Sure, there were some big-hitters doing the rounds and you would get an odd one spring up with a quirky sweep, a late dab or a scoop, but the modern game's full of them and the change has come about through T20 cricket – be it franchise, domestic or international. Batsmen are belting it to all parts and forget putting somebody on the boundary when they do because they can hit it straight over their heads.

They not only have licence to play these audacious shots, of course, but licence to get out playing them, too. Think back to the 1987 World Cup and the uproar when Mike Gatting was dismissed playing a reverse sweep. It was viewed as irresponsible. Arguably, Gatt suffered for being ahead of his time because it's the norm now to turn to shots which promote the manipulation of the field. Buttler is a great exponent of this, as was Pietersen with his switch hits.

Switch-hitting carries controversy for me. Is the batsman right-handed or left-handed? I wouldn't have a clue, and for the purposes of lbw I just don't know how you interpret it.

What I do know, however, is that this Buttler-type of player is box office and the game has never been as vibrant as it is now. I've been at it 55 years since my county first-team debut and it's never been as good as it is now. The grounds are rammed. Twenty20 finals days are sold out more than 10 months in advance and innovation has captured the imagination.

With regard to the leadership of the team, did England stumble upon a great one-day captain when they decided to ditch Alastair Cook a matter of two months before the 2015 World Cup? Or was it a genius decision taken by the selection quartet of then head coach Peter Moores, James Whitaker, Mick Newell and Angus Fraser back in December 2014? Equally, for Andrew Strauss to retain him for the next four-year cycle of one-day cricket.

The best limited-overs cycle history in English history.

I am not sure anyone could have foreseen how good things could become and whatever transpired, however they arrived at the decision, it is undeniable that they got an absolute gem in Eoin Morgan, a brilliant player in his own right and as honest as the day is long with his team. No question either that his team play for him.

No doubt that he's been a coach's dream either for Trevor Bayliss and now Chris Silverwood because he runs things very much like an old-school captain would. He calls the shots and that allows coaches to coach. He also has an extraordinary calmness on the field. England take their time in bowling their overs and get fined every now and again, because he is very deliberate in what he does.

He never changes his demeanour or his approach to leadership. He is ice-cool, and I reckon that this is directly influenced by one of his other big interests. He is very well connected within the horse-racing fraternity, likes a punt, and if you're into that business you've got to be steely. No emotions up, no emotions down. You make a decision and back that decision. It's a consistent approach.

I feel he brings that into his own batting, too, and is calculated in the way that he can change a game. When he takes on the responsibility of 'Right, it's me, I've got to do this,' he has a high success rate. For example, twice in the winter of 2019–20 – once in New Zealand and then in South Africa – he struck 21-ball fifties in Twenty20 internationals, breaking the England record for the fastest and then matching it. He is a pocket battleship who doesn't take any shit from anybody and in my experience every team, even going back to school, has a cock of the dressing room. The bloke who is fearless and never gets riled. Who, when things get most tense, stays calm. There have been a few standouts in this regard. People always used to say to be careful not to take on Peter Willey because he was quiet but a tough bloke. Same with Morgan.

He's such an easy customer to interview from a broadcaster's perspective because he'll engage with the interviewer. Some modern players are such hard work, making it fairly plain that they don't want to be there. They're looking over your head, or shoulder, whereas Morgan engages with you in an articulate manner on the most mundane things. The interview at the toss is a good example. There are a series of staple questions: what you think of the conditions? What do you think of the pitch? Why've you done this? Why've you done that? It would be forgivable to go into autopilot. He doesn't. He tells you who is being left out and why. He's an absolute dream because he gets that he is talking not to Rob Key or Ian Ward or Nick Knight but the viewers at home.

To me the way Morgan got England to play was totally un-English. And it might be no accident that the lad is actually Irish. Back in May 2015, he gave the team a stage on which to perform, told them to accept no limits, and he's not moved from it. And he has been decisive in wanting players in certain positions.

Before he put his stamp on the team, you could tell that opponents felt that they could control England. A side that would be conservative, keep wickets in hand and have a go in the last 10 overs, bowl to a formula. He changed all that and if you remember, a little mantra of his early days was 'no-fear cricket'.

And his commitment to it all has been 100 per cent. I hear people say that he should be playing for Ireland. Well, he decided his career path as a teenager, and if you listen to him he will tell you that he has lived in London longer than he did Dublin. Of course, he's made a good living out of it, and it has been richly deserved, having thrown in his lot with England yonks ago on the back of spending some time as a schoolboy at Dulwich College.

Accusations of poaching other countries' players are often levelled at the ECB but, as has been the case with the many South Africans who have come over seeking what they perceive as greater opportunities, it is the player who holds the aces. There's nobody actively lobbying players elsewhere, with offers of 'Oh, come and play for us.'

Morgan's my kind of bloke. One with a real work hard, play hard attitude. When it's celebration time he's always the last to leave. He's just a great leader and when he retires I would favour him being kept on in some sort of management role if he is that way inclined. Somehow I doubt that will be the case as he has lots of other interests, but his views would certainly carry some clout.

Morgan embodies all the good things about the England team that won the country's first 50-over title in 44 years of trying, and no one is bigger than that team, as was emphasised in a Twenty20 victory over New Zealand in Napier less than four months later.

Dawid Malan had just scored an unbeaten 103, only the

second hundred by an England batsman in the format, but Morgan couldn't have cared less about the size of the contribution. It was Malan's refusal to run a bye off the final ball for fear of being run out that irked him. He didn't like that one bit and the fact that Morgan brought it up unprompted in a press conference got a coded message across – don't be selfish. He didn't use those words, but his point was clear. Forget individual accolades and averages because the team could always do with that extra one run.

It might have seemed odd given that the hundred, plus 91 from Morgan, had taken the team total to 241 but it was about the setting of and adhering to the highest standards. I watched that innings of Malan's and it was out of this world. He played fantastically well and I was initially shocked when I heard the response from the captain. I was expecting him to receive plaudits; instead he got a flea in the ear. In addition to talking indirectly to Malan, though, he was also reinforcing to the rest of the squad and giving notice to anyone else hoping to break into that squad that no one would ever be bigger than the group. Then, when the team switched to South Africa the other side of Christmas, Malan was not considered to merit a place in the first-choice XI. Some would describe it as clinical to axe someone with six fifty-plus scores in nine T20 internationals; others brutal.

He's made some other tough decisions, too. I am thinking about David Willey, in particular, in the build-up to the 2019 World Cup. The problem for England was a nice one in that Jofra Archer was always going to be picked for that tournament once he had served his residency period and that meant someone had to miss out when they selected the final 15-man squad. You simply cannot ignore that kind of pace.

What a gentleman Willey was in the way he handled it, though. Shit happens, that's professional sport. He didn't make the cut and had to watch at home like the rest of us. And in case anyone was wondering whether or not Morgan cares for sentiment, consider the treatment of Liam Plunkett post-tournament. The fifth-most prolific seam bowler in the previous four-year cycle, the man whose three-wicket performance turned the tide of the final, and still one of the fittest members of the team, cast aside at the age of 34 for younger models like Sam Curran, Saqib Mahmood and Chris Jordan.

Although Morgan was 33 when he became England's first World Cup-winning captain, I wasn't surprised when he decided against walking away into the sunset because it was a case of unfinished business. It was heartening to hear he wants to play in the next two T20 World Cups. It's important that he's there for the next two shots at global glory. Both for him and the team. He can still produce end-of-innings devastation with his power hitting – only West Indies' Andre Russell can beat his 225 strike rate in the past 18 months.

And if he was to move aside upon the conclusion of the second of those tournaments in 2021, it would still allow a new captain 15 months at the helm ahead of the next 50-over World Cup in India, should he decide he cannot make it that far.

It has served England very well to have a Test captain and a limited-overs captain in recent years and there be no threat felt from one to the other. Neither has had designs on the other's job, and Morgan and Joe Root have got on fabulously. They are also good plotters, bouncing off each other, and I noted how during the period of inactivity caused by the coronavirus that Root spoke of how he looked up to Morgan. In years gone by, the Test captain would pull rank in this regard. Not any more. Some of that is undoubtedly down to the personality of Root.

Joe Root is the lad next door. The kind of chap you'd want your daughter to marry (yes, I know he is spoken for, Carrie). But he is a real family-oriented bloke, and you see his mum and dad, Helen and Matt, regularly at matches. They just blend in. Younger brother Billy is the livelier one whereas Joe is far more measured. He is just an all-round good guy.

He is not, I would argue, a typical bloke from Yorkshire. Now before I get a torrent of abuse from the dozens of folk from the Broad Acres who have invested in this book – time, that is, in asking friends if they can borrow it, rather than money – I live in Yorkshire. I love it to bits. I think it's great. And the people are forthright. Joe doesn't fit the mould.

And he's got a bit of mischief in him. I refer to the fact that he seems to like putting disguises on. First, there was that time in Birmingham's Walkabout night spot ahead of the 2013 Ashes when he stuck that wig on, things got a bit lively and David Warner was reprimanded for giving him a crack. Or that brilliant TV moment, just after the Ashes had been regained at Trent Bridge in 2015, when he put the Albert Einstein mask on and mimicked the late, great Bob Willis.

Those are great moments when you are in the dressing room and you've won. You can relax and be yourself. That's exactly what he was. In a few minutes of television, everyone got to see what England's batting hero on the field was like off it. I am sure that made a lasting impression on people.

He has a diplomatic side to him, too, and that means he is a very well-respected cricketer when it comes to other international teams. For a start, he has a good rapport with Kane Williamson of New Zealand. He's approachable, easy to speak to, easy to get on with, and a credit as captain of England, accepting that responsibility in much the same way that somebody like Graham Gooch did. Gooch viewed the position as a tremendous honour.

There has been some conjecture about Root's suitability for the role: has it had an adverse effect on his batting? Does he possess the tactical acumen? How does he handle his bowlers?

My assessment is that he is growing into captaincy. That's a process, as I know from my own experience; it takes time. The same for Michael Atherton, Nasser Hussain and Andrew Strauss.

Most importantly as a captain, you need a bowling attack. And he's just getting an attack now, particularly with the emergence of Jofra Archer. He needs to find out what makes Archer tick. Then he's got Mark Wood up his sleeve. He won't be fit every game but gives everything when he plays. Those two represent significant attacking weapons because of their extreme pace. Any captain can only be truly judged on the strength of his bowling attack because you need 20 wickets to win. Such an attack is coming together behind Jimmy Anderson and Stuart Broad.

There is also evidence that England's Test batting line-up is just settling down after a sustained period of volatility. Ideally you would like to unearth a top six as dependable and as of high a quality as that of the team that Andrew Strauss captained a decade ago. That sextet from the 2010–11 Ashes-winning era of Strauss, Alastair Cook, Jonathan Trott, Kevin Pietersen, Ian Bell and Paul Collingwood provided an amount of runs that aren't easily covered.

Now, after years of chopping and changing, of players coming and going, it looks as if in Rory Burns and Dominic Sibley they are going to get an opening pair. Zak Crawley is coming through pretty quickly, too, and someone like Dan Lawrence, of Essex, made a strong impression on England Lions' tour of Australia in early 2020. The first stage will be to allow it some time to settle down and allow players to bed in for the likes of Root, Stokes, Bairstow and Buttler to work with.

Root has always been destined for the top. When Graham Thorpe, who was one of our lads when I was England coach, first started his own coaching career, he went out to coach New South Wales in Australia's Sheffield Shield to broaden his education. People forget that. But he came back and worked his way through over here with England's pathway players.

I remember asking him: 'Who's coming through?' One word came back as an answer: R-O-O-T. Lad from Yorkshire. Top player. Only later did I become aware of his back story, being from Sheffield Collegiate, Michael Vaughan's old club.

Naturally, Vaughan took him under his wing. These days there seems to be regular conflict between members of the England team and Vaughan, who is quite outspoken as a critic, and the man in the middle of all this is Root. You cannot, if you are Joe Root, fail to respect what Vaughan did for England as an historic Ashes-winning captain, so he will feed off him. Equally, Vaughan has a job to do. He's a media person now and says what he thinks. Although he was born in Lancashire, he's a Yorkshireman deep down and there's that great maxim about a Yorkshireman: he says what he likes and he likes what he says.

One of the influences on Root from Vaughan are the funky fields he sets. It's not the regimented two slips and a gully. Catchers are often positioned at straight, short mid-on, on the drive at extra cover and round the corner for leg-side flicks. These kinds of variations were a Vaughan trait.

As for his individual game, Root knows what suits him best and he wants to bat at four. For me, he's a number four all day long. Why? I don't think he looks like a number three. Let me use a familiar template as a contrast. There is nothing of Jonathan Trott in him and he was England's best number three for some time. To me, Root looks like a four. Another template. He looks more like Kevin Pietersen, a busy player. Root's at his best when he's busy at the crease. His demeanour, his approach, he is a nailed-on number four. Not a first-drop technician.

I know there is that theory about playing your best player at three but to my mind that's a big Australian thing. Of course, in Australia the pitches are flatter, the Kookaburra ball has got no real seam on it and doesn't do as much as the Dukes does over here and teams stack up scores of 400–500 regularly.

Greg Chappell and Ricky Ponting were positioned at three because they were deemed the best batsmen Australia possessed at said times, but there's a pattern now and that is that the three best players in the world are at four.

In Test cricket, Steve Smith has batted at four either side of his year-long ban for the ball-tampering saga, most recently behind Marnus Labuschagne, and Virat Kohli is in the same position for India, coming in after Cheteshwar Pujara.

Root's biggest frustration will be that he's not converting fifties to hundreds – a ratio of 17 out of 65 by the start of the 2020 domestic season was just too low for a player of his standing – so until he improves it, he is not going to be talked about in that same breath as Smith and Kohli. I have no doubt that he will put this right. It's just something that you can go through as a player. In his case, there's no real reason for it happening. It's not as though he's fat and getting fatigued, it's not that he doesn't concentrate. That he's run out of steam. That he isn't good enough. He clearly is and so I reckon he'll come with an absolute burst in the second half of his career.

That last prediction carries significance because my view is that Root is yet to reach his peak. He has just entered his 30th year and so for me he is still a couple of years away. When he gets there, that will be the point at which he really starts to shake that conversion rate up.

When he struck a double hundred in the drawn Test match versus New Zealand in Hamilton in the autumn of 2019, it was only the sixth time in 28 he had got to three figures after reaching 50, a drop on his career return.

Don't forget, though, Michael Hussey, that fine Australian batsman, didn't start playing Test cricket until he was 30, the age Root turns on the penultimate day of 2020. People argue he averaged 52 before he was captain and his average has dipped considerably since. There's no debate about that but I just see it as the human element of captaincy. He will come again with that amount of talent. He will work it out. He's in a bit of a bad trot and still averaging in excess of 48. Hundreds of international cricketers would settle for that.

Modern England are in very good hands, I believe, with this dual leadership and the team is very much a representation of the country. This is very much a multicultural side and all the better for it.

After winning the World Cup, Eoin Morgan spoke of his pride in the diversity of the team. 'Allah was with us,' Morgan said in the final's post-match press conference. I think it's great to show that cricketers with South Asian backgrounds have a big part to play in the future of the England team. Adil Rashid and Moeen Ali are like team leaders in this regard.

Not being in the dressing room, we're not privy to what goes on but from what we hear, Moeen is the joker in the pack. Brother Mo, as they call him, and his mate Adil are like two peas in a pod. Wherever one is, the other is sure to be, and in my privileged position on the outfield before a game, at the start of Sky Sports' coverage, I always want to chat with these two because they're a real hoot. As a comedy act they could be as good as Ant and Dec or Morecambe and Wise, and Mo loves to play on the fact that his pal is not one of the brightest.

For example, on the 2018 tour of New Zealand there was an England team quiz night and ex-players were invited. A charity do organised by Jimmy Anderson and Stuart Broad, we were all placed into different teams and it was carefully scripted. They clearly wanted certain people in certain categories. That much was obvious when they began getting individuals up for specialist rounds.

They made Moeen the quizmaster for the spelling round and, funnily enough, Adil was one of those called up. As was Sam Curran. They were having to spell words like rhythm, February and necessary. Moeen moved along the line slickly but every time he got to Adil, just as he was about to open his mouth, there would be a shake of his head and he would say 'no,' moving on to the next person. Every time. It brought the house down.

One of the other rounds was not a test of knowledge at all. Rather, a physical challenge in which you had to clench a coin between your arse cheeks and manoeuvre yourself to drop it into a pint pot. Naturally, they had me lined up for that. I didn't fancy my chances much. Less so when I realised a rival competitor had turned up commando-style. It was really messy . . .

These are two lads at the heart of the England team, extremely popular in the dressing room and great role models for the Asian community on the field.

Adil is fiercely protective of Bradford. I suppose someone has to be! Perhaps England should host some Test matches there because he is someone who wants to play Test match cricket but not county cricket. That's a shame because the England selectors will struggle to select him on that basis, and for me he is the best leg-spinner in the world. He's got all the tools: a great temperament, the slider, a good googly and the leg-spinner.

Moeen will come again. He needed a break but he can be of real value to England. You have to admire the way that he's made himself into an off-spinner as a senior cricketer. And not any old off-spinner but one with in excess of 180 Test wickets. He's done a lot of listening and practising, particularly with Mushtaq Ahmed and Saqlain Mushtaq. It's not easy being a finger-spinner in modern-day cricket. Not easy at all and when he first started bowling for England, he hadn't done much of it in county cricket.

People forget how hard he worked at his game to become a threat. He's not the same type of bowler as his fellow off-spinner Nathan Lyon. Lyon is tall, wiry, a nice over-the-top spinner – and because of his release point tends to get more bounce than Moeen, who is more of a slider with his trajectory. Moeen arguably turns it more, though, and, despite a couple of batterings against Australia and India that will have undoubtedly dented his confidence, he is as good as we have got and invaluable to England in all formats when he's on form.

Not least for his batting. They have batted him everywhere – number nine, number eight, five, three; he's even opened and he'll still do a job. When he is playing with a smile on his face, he can be devastating.

Take that 53-ball hundred versus West Indies in Bristol at the end of the 2017 season, when he wowed with the sweet timing and distance he got on his sixes. Or the 39 off 11 balls he casually struck in the last-ball Twenty20 win over South Africa in Durban in 2020.

Moeen exemplifies what this current England team is about, and this England team plays with smiles on their faces. They have a lot of fun, and they win a lot of matches.

Just as Sir Donald Bradman represents the best the game has seen from an individual perspective, arguably no team has provided an entertainment factor to match the levels they have scaled as a white-ball outfit over the last five years. The love they have for playing the game shines through and they have a connection with the people. They have shown that the same principles I first learnt as a young boy at Accrington can be applied more than half a century later and it need not be necessary to alter attitude when ambition is increased.

They've shown that those with great characters can be great cricketers, too. That they can be, as a world title conveys, the best.

ACKNOWLEDGEMENTS

In the style of a contestant chatting to Ken Bruce on BBC Radio 2's Pop Master, I would like to thank the following: all the wonderful people I have met in cricket without whom this book would not have been possible, those who have been involved in its production, particularly Ian Marshall and his team at Simon & Schuster, Neil Fairbrother and Phoenix Management, Richard Gibson . . . and anybody else that knows me.

INDEX